insight text guide

Timothy Roberts

Great Expectations

Charles Dickens

First published in 2009, reprinted with minor amendments in 2019, 2020.

Insight Publications Pty Ltd
3/350 Charman Road
Cheltenham VIC 3192
Australia
Tel: +61 3 8571 4950
Fax: +61 3 8571 0257
Email: books@insightpublications.com.au

www.insightpublications.com.au

National Library of Australia Cataloguing-in-Publication entry:
Roberts, Timothy.
Charles Dickens' great expectations : insight text guide / Timothy Roberts.
9781921411021 (pbk.)
Insight text guides
Bibliography.
For secondary school age.
Dickens, Charles, 1812–1870. Great expectations.
823.8

Other ISBNs:
9781922378460 (digital)
9781922378477 (bundle: print + digital)

Cover design by Gisela Beer, based on a concept by The Modern Art Production Group

Printed in Australia by Ligare

contents

CHARACTER MAP

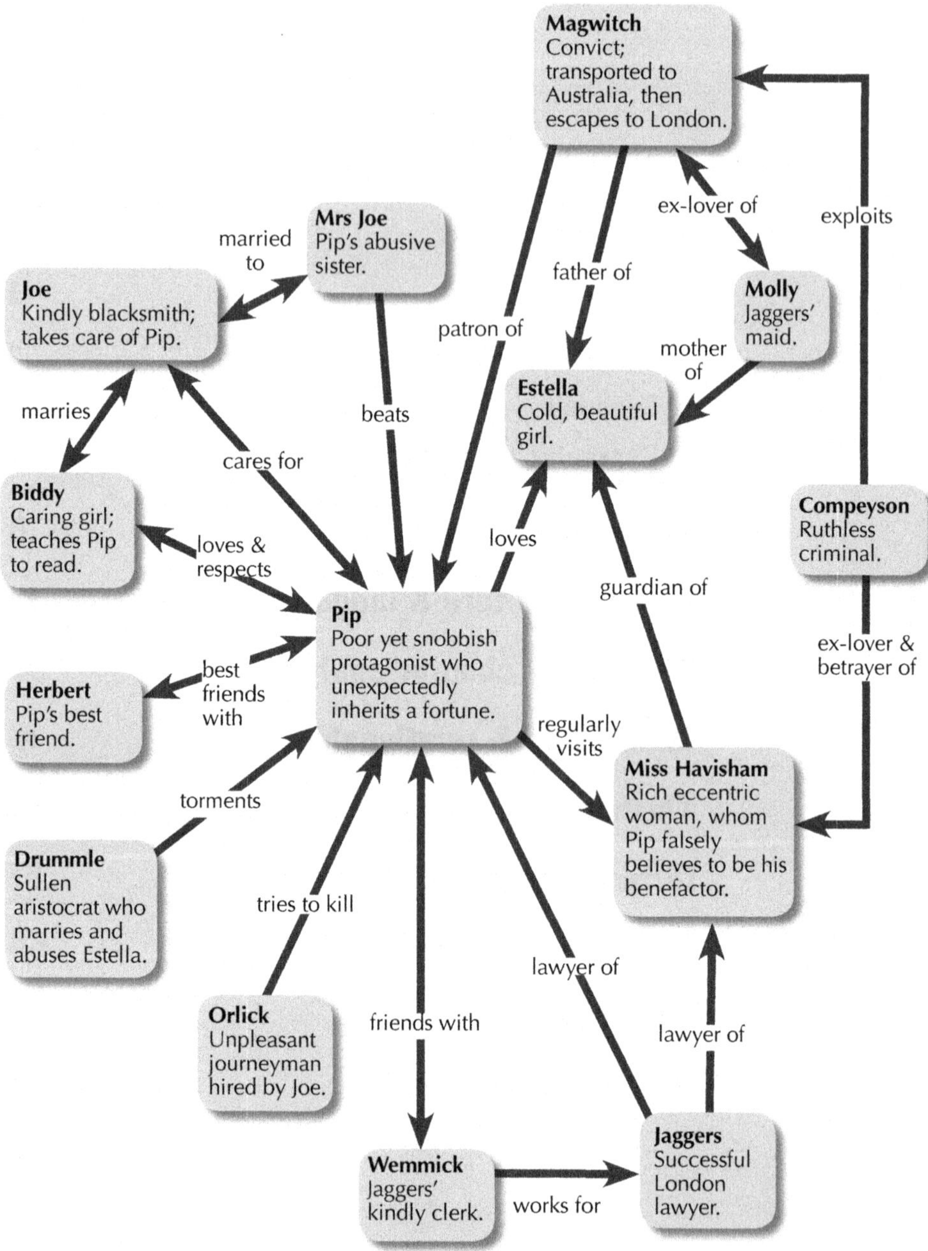

OVERVIEW

About the author

Charles Dickens was the best-known author of the 19th century. Born into a wealthy family in Portsmouth, England, in 1812, Dickens' early childhood was relatively comfortable. This was not to last, as his father was incarcerated in a prison for bankrupts when Charles was eight. To earn enough for the family to live on, eight-year-old Charles was pulled out of school and sent to work in a shoe polish factory for several months, often working shifts of more than 10 hours. This demeaning work scarred the young Dickens so deeply that he was later unable to complete his autobiography due to the pain of recalling these early memories. However, he included many autobiographical elements in his fiction, especially *David Copperfield* and *Great Expectations*.

Dickens' first adult job was as a court stenographer, after which he became a political correspondent with the *Morning Chronicle* newspaper. While there, he began to publish short, witty sketches under the pseudonym 'Boz'. These immensely popular pieces led to the serial publication of Dickens' first novel, *The Pickwick Papers*, a madcap chronicle of English life which made him an instant celebrity and attracted thousands of new readers to the paper. Dickens was just 22 years old.

By the time of his second novel, *Oliver Twist*, Dickens had become 'the closest the 19th century had to a pop star' (Swift 2007). Vast crowds of people would stand on the docks in Europe and America, waiting for the latest instalment of his works to arrive by boat. He had a powerful emotional hold over his readers; for example, his decision to kill off the child protagonist of his novel *The Old Curiosity Shop* plunged many of his dedicated readers into grief.

Dickens was extremely prolific, publishing 14 complete novels during his long and successful career, including such classics as *Nicholas Nickleby* (1838–39), *David Copperfield* (1849–50) and *Bleak House* (1852–53). He also published numerous essays and short stories, two travel books and several works of nonfiction, amounting to millions of published words in total.

The ageing Dickens became increasingly sombre as his domestic life began to disintegrate. After the failure of his marriage in 1858, he began an affair with the young stage actress Ellen Tiernan which scandalised many. His professional life, meanwhile, remained as busy as ever. Beginning in 1866, Dickens began his famous 'reading tours', in which he would act out well-known scenes from his works for adoring crowds. These tremendously popular tours were so gruelling that they are said to have contributed to his premature death at the age of 57. Dickens was buried, against his wishes, in Poet's Corner at Westminster Abbey.

Synopsis

Volume 1

Pip, a poor orphan, lives in desolate marsh country with his abusive elder sister and her kindly blacksmith husband, Joe. One day he is accosted by an escaped convict demanding food and a file. Pip steals these items from his house to placate the convict, who briefly escapes before being recaptured. For the rest of his life, Pip is haunted by guilt for helping the convict escape.

One day, Pip, who is being apprenticed to Joe, is summoned to the mansion of Miss Havisham, a wealthy and eccentric woman. While there, Pip falls in love with Miss Havisham's foster-daughter, a beautiful yet cruel girl named Estella, who chides him about his working-class coarseness. Pip becomes dissatisfied with his humble life and yearns to become wealthy in order to be worthy of her love. Tragedy strikes the household when Pip's sister is violently assaulted and left insensible. After this traumatic event, she does not bother Pip or Joe anymore.

On the verge of completing his apprenticeship, Pip discovers that he has anonymously been left a fortune. He soon becomes disdainful towards Joe, as well as towards the kindly and caring Biddy, who has come to care for his sister. Pip incorrectly guesses that his benefactor is Miss Havisham, concluding that she intends him to become Estella's husband. Dreaming of a future with Estella, the newly wealthy Pip terminates his apprenticeship and eagerly leaves for London to start his new life as a gentleman.

Volume 2

In London, Pip begins to cultivate the bad habits of a wealthy and idle young man. As he slowly learns that Estella does not return his feelings, Pip's love for her develops into an unhealthy obsession. Soon Pip's sister dies and he is called back for her funeral. He briefly stays at the forge, but quickly leaves again after insulting Joe and Biddy.

Pip has an unwelcome visit from Magwitch, the convict he assisted on the marshes. He is in danger from the authorities for illegally returning to England, after having been transported to Australia following the encounter with Pip in the marshes years ago. Magwitch reveals to Pip that he, not Miss Havisham, is the true source of Pip's fortune.

Volume 3

Although initially shocked by this news, Pip gradually begins to feel affection for Magwitch and tries unsuccessfully to help him escape from the police. On Magwitch's arrest, Pip loses his fortune. Realising the folly of his obsession with Estella, he confronts Miss Havisham about her savage treatment of the girl. Miss Havisham admits that she has used Estella as a tool to wreak revenge on men for being jilted at the altar years before. Soon after, Pip discovers that Estella is Magwitch's illegitimate daughter.

At the novel's conclusion, a chastened Pip returns to the blacksmith's forge to apologise to Biddy and Joe, who are now about to be married, and returns some years later to visit their children. On leaving the forge a final time, he meets Estella – who has just been freed from a violent marriage – and tentatively reconciles with her. At the conclusion, their future together remains uncertain.

Character summaries

Pip

'I want to be a gentleman ... I am not at all happy as I am. I am disgusted with my calling and with my life' (p.127). The narrative begins when the protagonist Pip is six years old and ends when he is around 34. Pip is a self-centred character who betrays his true friends after being blinded by the lure of money. After a series of painful events, he eventually comes to understand the value of friendship.

Joe

'Pip, dear old chap, life is made of ever so many partings welded together' (p.224). The compassionate blacksmith Joe protects his nephew Pip from his violent sister. Although Pip callously rejects Joe after becoming wealthy, Joe never loses his faith in Pip. The two eventually reconcile at the conclusion.

Mrs Joe

'Who brought you up by hand?' (p.9). Mrs Joe, Pip's violent elder sister, torments Pip throughout his childhood. Chastened after her assault, she signals for Pip's forgiveness before she dies.

Magwitch

'If I ain't a gentleman, nor yet ain't got no learning, I'm the owner of such' (p.321). The convict Magwitch is saved by Pip at the beginning of the novel and anonymously donates the fortune that he makes in Australia to Pip in return. When Magwitch returns to London and reveals that he is Pip's benefactor, Pip is horrified; however, the two men soon reconcile and Pip helps orchestrate Magwitch's escape attempt. Magwitch is eventually captured by police, and dies in prison.

Mr Wopsle

'The gluttony of Swine is put before us, as an example to the young' (p.27). The vain Wopsle, a friend of Pip's sister, is a frustrated preacher who becomes an inept and unsuccessful stage actor.

Biddy

'I only want you to do well, and to be comfortable' (p.128). The kind Biddy teaches Pip to read and cares deeply for him; before Pip meets Estella, there is a subtle suggestion that they will fall in love. Although she is shy, Biddy criticises Pip for abandoning Joe, whom she eventually decides to marry.

Pumblechook

'This boy must be bound, out of hand. That's *my* way. Bound out of hand' (p.104). The fawning Pumblechook falsely claims to be Pip's 'benefactor', usurping the place of Pip's real carer, Joe, in the hope of profiting from Pip's fortune. Pip eventually learns to stand up to his vain and greedy uncle.

Jaggers

'"Now, I have nothing to say to you," said Mr Jaggers, throwing his finger at them' (p.167). Jaggers is a ferocious lawyer who, coincidentally, administers both Pip's inheritance and Miss Havisham's estate. He made his name by successfully defending Estella's mother against a murder charge. Jaggers is an extremely remote and patrician figure, his human warmth having been destroyed by the pressures of his job. However, he is highly trustworthy.

Wemmick

'... the office is one thing, and private life is another' (p.208). Jaggers' buttoned-down clerk, who betrays little emotion inside work hours, Wemmick is actually a caring individual who looks after his aged father and protects Pip when he is in danger. He conceals his caring private life from public view in order to come across as more ruthless than he really is.

Compeyson

'He'd no more heart than a iron file, he was as cold as death, and he had the head of the Devil …' (p.348). Compeyson, the other convict Pip meets on the marshes after encountering Magwitch, is a master criminal who manipulates others and evades justice through his amorality. Before Pip's life story begins, Compeyson jilts Miss Havisham at the altar and introduces the vulnerable Magwitch to a life of criminality.

Orlick

'You was always in Old Orlick's way since ever you was a child' (p.425). Joe's unrefined and violent assistant, Orlick represents everything that Pip despises. Intensely jealous of Pip, Orlick fatally assaults Pip's sister, pursues and intimidates Biddy, and unsuccessfully tries to murder Pip.

Bentley Drummle

'I wouldn't lend one of you a sixpence. I wouldn't lend anybody a sixpence' (p.215). The thuggish Drummle is another of Pip's enemies. He too torments Pip, infuriating him by marrying and then physically abusing Estella.

Estella

'I have no heart …' (p.237). Estella, Pip's romantic interest throughout his life, is abandoned by her parents as a baby and placed in the care of Miss Havisham. Miss Havisham destroys Estella's childhood; she starves Estella of affection and moulds her personality as a way of wreaking revenge on the male sex. Trained to be an uncaring sadist all her life, Estella is consequently unable to feel genuine affection for others.

Miss Havisham

'I stole her heart away and put pure ice in its place' (p.399). A bitter and eccentric woman who dedicates her later life to brainwashing her foster-daughter, Estella, Miss Havisham becomes a recluse after being jilted at the altar in her youth. For many years, Pip mistakenly thinks that she is his benefactor. Although she wrongs Pip by turning Estella against him, she gains Pip's forgiveness before her death.

Herbert Pocket

'"But the thing is," said Herbert Pocket, "that you look about you. *That's* the grand thing"' (p.184). Herbert, Pip's best friend and room-mate, is a trusting and rather passive young man who supports Pip throughout the story. Pip's high regard for Herbert is shown when he uses some of the money received from his inheritance to help Herbert enter a career.

Startop

'Startop had been spoilt by a weak mother and kept at home when he ought to have been at school …' (p.203). Startop is a reserved person who attends the 'Finches of the Grove' club with Pip, Drummle and Herbert. He is a dependable but rather nondescript friend, whose most important role is helping Magwitch escape by boat.

BACKGROUND & CONTEXT

The settings of *Great Expectations*

Dickens took care to reproduce real-life settings accurately in his fiction, and many settings in *Great Expectations* demonstrate his meticulous attention to detail. Pip's London is carefully modelled on the city as it was during the early part of the 19th century. The rural locations are less factually based. While they are recognisable as the Thames estuaries, and many villages, such as Gravesend, are based on real places, Dickens also invents several wholly fictional locations – most notably Wemmick's bizarre castle-like house at Walworth and Miss Havisham's mansion. The geographic terrain of the novel, then, is constructed of a hybrid of fact and fiction that are woven together into a seamless whole.

The novel's rural locations are very clearly set apart from the urban locations. In broad terms, the country represents Pip's childhood, while the city represents his adolescence. Pip's departure from the country for the city at the beginning of his teenage years coincides with his impending adolescence, suggesting that his physical journey to the city doubles as a spiritual rite of passage.

The division between rural and urban is moral as well as physical. Dickens often associates the country with purity and simplicity, and the city with corruption and decay. Although bad things do happen in the country – Pip's first encounter with Magwitch, for example, as well as his later encounter with Orlick both occur on the marshes – the city of London itself is generally singled out as the major source of the novel's corruption. The contrast between the two worlds is reflected in their opposing physical natures: while the rural locations are generally sparse and barren, London is 'ugly, crooked, narrow and dirty' (p.163).

The London of two centuries ago is, of course, very different from the London of our own time. Far from the largely affluent city it is today, many parts of London in the early 19th century were mired in abject poverty and squalor. Dickens was acutely aware of the grim fate of the underprivileged in London, who lived without adequate sanitation or medical treatment in what were then known as 'slums'; they also did not enjoy the support of charities as we would recognise them today. In his journalism as well as in his fiction, Dickens frequently spoke out against this intolerable situation in an attempt to encourage those in power to improve the city's appalling living conditions.

The Origin of Species

Dickens' pessimistic view of society suggests that he had read Charles Darwin's highly influential book, *The Origin of Species*, which was published shortly before *Great Expectations* began to appear in the journal *All the Year Round*. It is hard to imagine the impact of Darwin's book today. At the time of its publication, most English people believed, in public at least, that God created the world according to a harmonious 'divine plan'. Darwin upended this theory by claiming that nature is in fact ruled by godless forces that only *appear* harmonious. Nature's driving principle was not cooperation, as would be expected in a divinely created world, but *competition*. Nature, said Darwin, always involved a ruthless struggle between competitors for scarce resources.

Although *The Origin of Species* doesn't directly discuss human societies, people soon applied Darwin's bleak-sounding theories of competition and natural selection to human nature. *Great Expectations'* social vision seems to reflect this pessimistic view because it strongly suggests that society is governed by greed and avarice rather than by harmony and cooperation.

The Industrial Revolution

Although Dickens does not provide any exact dates for *Great Expectations*, critics have pinpointed Pip's birth to near the beginning of the 19th century (Sadrin 1999, p.540). This would place the novel's opening shortly after the beginning of the Industrial Revolution, which began in late 18th-century England. The term refers to Britain's rapid transition from an agricultural to a manufacturing society. While the book is set before railways and other major technological developments were introduced, Pip lives in a world that has already been changed drastically by industry. His journey from a rural to an urban environment echoes thousands of similar journeys taken by labourers at that time who flooded into London looking for work in the hellish factories that were then springing up all over the city. This massive exodus from the country to the city caused London's population to explode: in 1801 its population was under one million, while by 1821 it had reached almost 1.4 million (London Online) – a 50 per cent increase in a very short period. The already crowded city was placed under immense strain. Without proper sanitation, it wasn't a healthy place to live, either: life expectancy in London was just *29 years* in 1829 – much lower than it was in rural areas – mainly due to the combination of a crushing population density and open sewers (Daunton 2004).

The problem of criminality and transportation

Along with the rise in urban poverty came a significantly increased crime rate. However, punishment practices for criminals had changed substantially in the second half of the 18th century as fewer and fewer crimes were deemed worthy of the death penalty, which was becoming increasingly rare during the time that *Great Expectations* was set. Instead of being routinely executed, as they had been previously, many serious criminals began to be imprisoned instead. Yet London's dangerously overcrowded prisons were not up to the task (Hudson 1998, p.209). A temporary solution was found by housing prisoners in rotting, decommissioned sailing ships called 'hulks', which were anchored offshore. Pip's family discusses the hulks (p.14) and Magwitch and Compeyson escape from one in the opening chapter.

Transporting prisoners to British colonies proved to be a more convenient long-term solution – according to the 'out of sight, out of mind' principle at least! The first boatload of convicts arrived in Australia in 1788. Magwitch is sentenced to 14 years' hard labour in Botany Bay for his crimes. (Transportation sentences to Australia generally lasted either seven or 14 years, depending on the severity of the crime.) Convicts who had served their sentences were permitted to become landholders in their place of transportation, and Magwitch was able to become wealthy in this manner after serving his sentence. However, there was one condition to this rule: convicts who had served their sentences were forbidden ever to return to England. By breaking this rule, Magwitch automatically becomes eligible for the death penalty.

The treatment of children

When we are introduced to Pip, he is visiting the graves of his five dead brothers, all of whom died in infancy. Such a horrific death rate was common in 19th-century England, where children often bore the brunt of unsanitary conditions and exploitative work practices.

The treatment of children changed drastically for the worse at the beginning of the 19th century. To satisfy the Industrial Revolution's insatiable demand for factory labourers, children were sent to work in coal mines or factories: William Blake, in his poem 'Jerusalem', bitterly named these the 'Dark Satanic Mills'. The casualties were huge. Chimneysweeps as young as five, for example, would often die of testicular cancer from the carcinogens contained in soot; the disease was nicknamed 'soot cancer' because of this (Shors 2004, p.244). In comparison to many less fortunate children of the time, Pip would have been very lucky to be a blacksmith's apprentice!

This intolerable situation took a long time to change. It only began to improve when new child protection laws were passed in 1833 and 1844, limiting the number of hours that children could work. It was not until 1878 that the employment of children under 10 was banned outright. By drawing attention to these horrible abuses through his fiction and journalism, Dickens played a major role in helping to eliminate child labour, even though it was not completely abolished until after his death.

Great Expectations frequently deals with the mistreatment of children. Pip is routinely physically abused by his sister and humiliated, or tormented by other adults that he meets. Many of Dickens' novels feature abused or neglected children, including the child prostitute Martha in *David Copperfield* and the destitute crossing sweeper Tom in *Bleak House*. This issue was Dickens' greatest concern, and he dealt with it virtually throughout his career.

Publishing context – serial publication

Unlike today, where novelists usually publish their works in a single bound volume, most popular writers in the mid 19th century published in magazines that came in weekly or monthly instalments. While Dickens strongly felt that publishing single-volume works 'held the key to immortality' (Rosenberg 1999, p.403), he owed his popularity to cheap serial publication, which enabled him to reach a massive audience for a small price. These affordable magazines – along with circulating libraries, which blossomed in the 19th century – allowed Dickens' fiction to be enjoyed by all sections of the public for the first time.

Serial publication also shaped the *structure* of Dickens' novels. Writing successfully in instalments, like writing for television serials, requires a 'cliffhanger' style that leaves the reader in suspense until the next issue. The last chapter of each instalment of *Great Expectations* ends with an exciting or suspenseful scene. For example, the second monthly instalment of *Great Expectations* ends when Pip leaves for London to begin his new life.

Dickens did not complete his novels before the first instalments were published. By shaping his stories month by month, Dickens was able to be more flexible as a writer than he would have been if he had published the work in a single volume. Most famously, the ending of *Great Expectations* was changed at the last minute, after Dickens' friend Bulwer-Lytton – now best known for writing the immortal words 'It was a dark and stormy night' – criticised it for being too dreary. (You can judge for yourself, as the original ending is included with the Penguin Classics edition.)

Although Dickens benefited from serial publication, he disliked some aspects of the practice. Most of all, he was worried that it made him seem more like an 'entertainer' than an 'artist'. Just as many critics today call all soap operas 'trash', Dickens' contemporaries often had a negative, even snobbish, opinion of serially published novels. Dickens was right to be worried about his reputation, too, as he was seen mostly as a popular entertainer until a long time after his death. It was only in the mid 20th century, when his novels began being studied in university courses, that his reputation as an artist slowly began to grow.

GENRE, STRUCTURE & LANGUAGE

Great Expectations can be seen as a 'hybrid' novel because it blends many different genres. In this section, we will look at several of the major genres used by Dickens to create this unusual work.

The bildungsroman

Great Expectations shares many features with the bildungsroman, a German word meaning 'novel of development'. This genre, which became popular in 18th-century Germany, remains one of the most enduring genres in literature and film. Many bildungsromans, including *Great Expectations*, involve a 'rags-to-riches' plot. These types of stories are almost always *optimistic*, because they suggest that anyone – even someone from a disadvantaged background – can become successful.

Although *Great Expectations* features a poor protagonist who becomes rich, it is very pessimistic about the effects of 'class mobility', which refers to the opportunity for individuals to move up into a different social class. Pip's inheritance, instead of making him happy, seems to corrupt him and ultimately make him more miserable than he was originally. The novel is also highly critical of the idea of ambition, another value that is generally praised in the bildungsroman. Just as Pip's money makes him unhappy, his powerful ambition only makes him more insecure.

The Gothic

Gothic novels, which were extremely popular in the mid 19th century, aimed to create a sense of fear by using dark, foreboding settings and supernatural or mysterious events. While realism deals with relatively normal situations, the Gothic deals with bizarre or disturbing ones. In contrast to the bildungsroman, which celebrates stories of life and growth, the Gothic focuses on stories of decay and death.

Although *Great Expectations* is not a pure Gothic novel, it does contain several distinctly Gothic elements. For example, Pip is surrounded by figures that resemble monsters. Miss Havisham, for example, is often described as a vampire. Pip sees her as 'corpse-like ... as if the admission of the natural light of day would have struck her to dust' (p.60). She also behaves like a vampire towards Estella, acting 'as though she were devouring the beautiful creature she had reared' (p.302). Miss Havisham thrives, in other words, by draining the life from others.

There are many other monstrous adults in the novel – Pip's sister, Compeyson and Magwitch are all described as terrifying threats to Pip's physical safety. Like a Gothic hero, Pip is frequently pursued by uncontrollable forces and plagued by nightmares and paranoia. The world around him often does not seem to work according to normal rules. It contains a series of wildly surreal and bizarre environments that can seem disconnected from one another, most notably Miss Havisham's dark, decaying mansion, where everything has been left as it was at the moment of her betrayal decades before. Pip is obsessed with the imagery of death: Magwitch, for example, looks to the young Pip as if 'he were eluding the hands of ... dead people' (pp.6–7).

The 'antihero'

The idea of the 'hero' of a story suggests a strong, admirable figure. In Greek tragedy, for example, the hero is almost always strong and brave, even though he is usually killed at the end. Even flawed heroes, such as Shakespeare's Hamlet, still have many positive qualities. Many popular novels also feature heroic characters. In one of the most famous, *Pride and Prejudice*, the stubborn yet intelligent Elizabeth falls in love with the proud yet compassionate Mr Darcy. Both of these characters are flawed, yet they are also admired by audiences for their many positive qualities.

Pip does not make an admirable hero. Although he bravely helps the convict at the very beginning of the story, he rarely acts heroically afterwards. The way in which he treats others, particularly his old friends, makes him seem especially unheroic. His many weaknesses, therefore, make him more of an 'antihero' than a hero. Unlike the hero, who exposes the flaws of society through his virtues, it is through Pip's flaws that we are able to understand the problems and contradictions inherent in his society. For example, Pip's class snobbery makes us aware of the wider problem of his society's patently unfair class system.

Realism

Great Expectations is frequently considered a realist novel. This might seem strange – after all, how can a story featuring a woman who stays indoors for over 20 years be considered in any way 'realistic'? Although the novel contains too many implausible events to be considered 'realistic' in this narrow sense, it does feature many elements of realism. Most importantly, it uses complex characters and highly detailed physical environments to create a convincing sense of reality. Although many events in *Great Expectations* are extraordinary or implausible, they are always described in a detailed and consistent manner.

Many, though not all, of the characters are 'realistic' in the sense that they are complex individuals with plausible motivations. To provide each character with a solid sense of individuality, Dickens generally introduces each one by describing their physical characteristics in detail. For example, Wemmick is 'a dry man, rather short in stature, with a square wooden face, whose expression seemed to have been imperfectly chipped out with a dull-edged chisel' (p.171). The characters remain consistent across time; even characters who age considerably over the course of the story retain some key mannerisms from their past – the click in Magwitch's throat, for example, remains constant throughout his life – just as real people can retain certain characteristics from their youth into adulthood.

Yet many of Dickens' characters are made more believable by their ability to change over time in response to to changing circumstances, just as real people tend to do. Among the novel's dynamic characters, Wemmick gradually becomes warmer and more human, Miss Havisham becomes more remorseful, and Magwitch changes from a terrifying convict to a comforting father figure. Other characters (Compeyson, for example) are static. In his classic study *Aspects of the Novel*, EM Forster refers to these two types of characters as 'round' and 'flat'.

Different voices

One of the most distinctive elements of Dickens' style is his ability to create distinctive voices for each of his characters. Every character speaks differently, and by reading a piece of dialogue, it is almost always possible to tell who is speaking. Compare the voices of two of the novel's uneducated characters, Joe and Magwitch. Both use language 'ungrammatically', yet each is very different. Magwitch speaks in an abrupt, aggressive manner ('Darn Me if I couldn't eat 'em!', p.4), while Joe speaks in a convoluted but endearing style ('I Bolted, myself, when I was your age – frequent – and as a boy I've been among many Bolters; but I never seen your Bolting equal yet, Pip', p.12).

Unreliable first-person narration

Because Pip narrates the story, we are restricted to his personal viewpoint. The first-person narrative style makes his experiences more immediate and sympathetic than they would be if they were narrated from a detached third-person perspective. The first-person narrative perspective in *Great Expectations* works so well because there are, in a sense, *two* narrators. Think about who *really* narrates the story – is it the younger Pip, who experiences the story's events, or the older Pip, who writes them down? It is a mixture of the two. We are not always sure which Pip – young or old – is speaking to us. Sometimes the young Pip tells his story uninterrupted, and we simply witness events through his eyes. For example, when Pip tries to disguise Magwitch from the police, he tells us that 'there was Convict in the very grain of the man' (p.337). As Pip is speaking about himself in the past tense here, we know that he is referring to a view that was held by his *younger* self (witnessing events), but is no longer held by his *older* self.

At other times, the older Pip intrudes directly on the narrative with his more experienced views. For example, when Pip tells us that 'All other swindlers upon earth are nothing to the self-swindlers, and with such pretences did I cheat myself' (p.225), his *older* self is lamenting the young Pip's lack of self-awareness. Two voices – the young, selfish

Pip and the older, kinder Pip – speak side by side throughout the story. Dickens implies that the older Pip's voice is reliable, while the younger Pip's is unreliable. However, the younger Pip's spontaneous voice is far more interesting and vital than the older Pip's more measured, careful voice. Both voices, then, have their distinctive characteristics, just as people view life's events differently at different ages.

Irony

Dickens uses these two different narrators to create *irony*, a bitter type of humour that often occurs when a person is experiencing events that they don't fully understand. For example, when Pip gets drunk at Pumblechook's house, he notes that his host seemed like 'a sensible practical good-hearted prime fellow' (p.155). This is obviously a bad judgement: we know that Pip only sees the utterly foolish Pumblechook as 'sensible' because he is drunk. The older Pip knows this, too. By letting the older narrator in on the joke, Dickens uses the young Pip's obviously mistaken opinion of Pumblechook to make an ironic point about his lack of judgement.

Surface structure – chronology

Great Expectations is presented in chronological order. The novel's main action occurs over approximately 16 years of Pip's life. Volume 1 covers Pip's life from age six to 18; Volume 2 from age 18 to 23; and Volume 3 mainly deals with Pip at age 23. The brief final chapter is set 11 years later, which would make Pip approximately 34 when he meets Estella at the conclusion (Sadrin 1999, p.538). This linear structure is punctuated by several flashbacks, which provide extra information about the lives of several important characters. Dickens' plan of the novel's chronology can be found on pages 509–11.

CHAPTER-BY-CHAPTER ANALYSIS

Volume 1

The first part of the novel covers Pip's life as a young boy. For the majority of this volume, Pip lives in an impoverished family. The volume ends with his inheritance of a fortune and his departure for London. Besides laying a foundation for the novel's 'rags-to-riches' story, the first volume provides important information about Pip's personality, depicting him as a child who suffers from feelings of anxiety and guilt.

Chapter 1 (pp.3–7)

Summary: *Pip encounters an escaped convict on the marshes.*

We meet Pip as a small, shivering boy visiting his parents' and siblings' graves on the bleak marshlands near his house. While he is meditating on the fate of his dead family, he is confronted by an escaped convict who demands food and a file. The opening is very dramatic and immediate, putting us straight into the middle of the action rather than starting with the character's birth, as a typical 19-century novel might. The sudden beginning shocks the audience into identifying with Pip by fearing for his safety.

Q How does Dickens convey Pip's unique first-person perspective in this scene?

Chapters 2–3 (pp.7–21)

Summary: *Pip steals food for the convict and delivers it to him.*

Pip returns home, where we meet his sister (a violent, cruel woman) and his brother-in-law, Joe (a kindly blacksmith). While at dinner, Pip guiltily steals some food for the convict. On his way to deliver the food, Pip meets a second convict more terrifying than the first. He manages to run away and deliver the requested items to the first convict. As the grateful convict eats and frees himself, Pip flees.

Key point

Pip's character is established as highly agitated and nervous in these opening chapters; he is continually fearful about something.

Q How does Joe try to protect Pip from his sister?

Q Did Pip do the right thing in helping the convict, or should he feel guilty?

Chapter 4 (pp.21–30)

Summary: *Christmas dinner at Pip's house is interrupted by a group of soldiers.*

At dinner with several of his sister's cruel friends (Pumblechook, Mr and Mrs Hubble, and Wopsle), Pip becomes increasingly terrified of his theft being discovered. He is saved by the abrupt intrusion of a group of soldiers, one of whom informs the household that there are escaped convicts nearby. The dinner scene subtly shows us the mindless abuse Pip suffers at the hands of nearly all the adult characters, with Joe as the exception. By drawing attention to the continued threat of discovery, Dickens puts us on Pip's side and against the adults.

Q How does Dickens use the threat of Pip's discovery to create suspense?

Chapters 5–6 (pp.30–42)

Summary: *The convicts are found.*

Pip, Joe and Wopsle set off with the soldiers in pursuit of the convicts, who are eventually found hiding together in a ditch. Magwitch, the convict aided by Pip, protects him by claiming responsibility for the theft. Back at the house, Pip remains silent about it.

Q How does Dickens create a contrast between the personalities of the two convicts?

Q How is Pip treated by the other adults in this scene?

Chapters 7–8 (pp.43–65)

Summary: *Pip begins his formal education, and is summoned by Miss Havisham.*

In these key chapters, Pip begins to learn to read, and pledges to pass his skills on to Joe in secret. He also develops a friendship with his tutor, Biddy. One day, he is unexpectedly summoned by Miss Havisham, a rich eccentric woman who lives nearby. At her mansion, Satis House, Pip is introduced to Miss Havisham and her foster-daughter Estella, a beautiful yet cold girl who insults Pip's impoverished background. Upon leaving, the frustrated Pip has a brief vision of Miss Havisham's death.

Key point

Miss Havisham's request for Pip's company is a turning point in his life. Pip is perfectly happy with his simple life before meeting her; yet he yearns to escape afterwards. Pip begins his slide into dissatisfaction after his first meeting with Estella, when his happily anticipated career as a blacksmith quickly becomes an unbearable burden.

Q How does Pip's sister react to Miss Havisham's request? Why?

Q Compare and contrast the characters of Estella and Biddy. Does Pip fall for Estella simply because she is beautiful?

Chapter 9 (pp.65–72)

Summary: *Pip returns home and tells his family about Miss Havisham.*

Vigorously questioned about Miss Havisham on his return, Pip makes up a series of lies about his time there. Struck by remorse afterwards, Pip privately admits to Joe that he was lying.

Q Why does Pip feel the need to lie about his time at Miss Havisham's?

Chapter 10 (pp.73–9)

Summary: *Pip learns to read, and meets a strange man.*

Pip's reading lessons with Biddy progress quickly, as he is now motivated by a desire to impress Estella. While at the Three Jolly Bargemen with Joe and Wopsle, Pip meets an ominous-looking man who secretly shows him the file Pip stole at the beginning of the novel. This man gives Pip two pounds. Pip is disturbed by the sight of him, and has a nightmare about the experience later.

Q What does Pip's nightmare signify?

Chapters 11–12 (pp.79–99)

Summary: *Pip visits Miss Havisham's over a period of several months.*

On a birthday visit to Miss Havisham's, Pip meets her greedy and fawning relatives and Mr Jaggers, her lawyer, who will later become Pip's guardian. Pip and Estella play cards; she beats him soundly and rejects his love. The dejected Pip walks into the garden, where he is challenged to, and wins, a fist fight with a young stranger; Estella permits Pip to kiss her as a reward. Although terrified of being punished for his violent act, Pip visits several more times and is finally asked to bring Joe back with him. Back at the forge, Pip confides to his tutor, Biddy, that he is in love with Estella.

Q What does the behaviour of Miss Havisham's relatives, especially Camilla, suggest about the attitude towards money in the novel?

Q How does Dickens portray Pip's steadily increasing unhappiness with his prospects at the forge?

Chapters 13–14 (pp.99–108)

Summary: *Miss Havisham buys Pip's apprenticeship, but he remains unhappy.*

Pip and Joe go to Miss Havisham's, where they find out that she wishes to pay Joe for Pip's apprenticeship. Privately, however, Pip now despises the trade. Having finished his formal education, Pip tries unsuccessfully to educate Joe, whom he feels increasingly contemptuous towards.

Key point

The seeds of doubt about his coarse ways (planted in Pip's mind by Estella in Chapter 8) sprout here. Pip's contempt for Joe is a serious betrayal, as Joe is his best friend.

Q Why doesn't Joe address Miss Havisham directly when he is speaking to her in Chapter 13?

Chapters 15–16 (pp.108–24)

Summary: *Mrs Joe is assaulted, and lies in a coma.*

Joe's sullen journeyman assistant, Orlick, is introduced. Pip returns to Miss Havisham's to thank her for her generosity. On his way home, he learns that more convicts have escaped from the hulks nearby. Pip arrives home to find that his sister has been violently attacked with a leg-iron, causing him to remember his earlier guilt over freeing Magwitch.

Key point

Pip's false impression that he 'must have had some hand in the attack' (p.120) repeats a pattern. Although he has not committed a crime, he consistently feels culpable for crimes committed by others.

Q How is the character Orlick described?

Q Why does Pip feel himself to be a 'more legitimate object of suspicion than any one else' (p.120)?

Chapters 17–18 (pp.124–46)

Summary: *After telling Biddy his aspirations of becoming a gentleman, Pip inherits his expectations and prepares for London.*

On his birthday, Pip revisits Mrs Havisham's. Back home, Pip tells Biddy – who has come to the forge to help care for Mrs Joe – about his love for Estella, while Biddy confides that Orlick has made unwanted advances toward her. In the fourth year of his apprenticeship, Pip is told by the lawyer Jaggers that he is the heir to a fortune. Joe, on hearing the news, agrees to free Pip from his obligations as an apprentice. Instead of being grateful, the newly wealthy Pip begins to act arrogantly towards Joe and Biddy.

Key point

Pip's 'dreams come true' – he looks forward to entering the new world of money and leaving his old life behind. The chapter also contains one of the mature Pip's many regretful comments about his earlier mistreatment of 'dear good Joe' (p.141). The gap between character and narrator widens, as young Pip rapidly becomes less sympathetic. It is already obvious that Pip's wealth will make him unhappy.

Q How is the possible attraction between Pip and Biddy raised?

Q In what ways does Pip's attitude towards his family change after he learns of his inheritance?

Chapter 19 (pp.146–60)

Summary: *Pip departs for London.*

Biddy angrily defends Joe when Pip says insulting things about him to her. Pip returns to Miss Havisham's to say goodbye, falsely presuming she is his benefactor. He becomes very nervous about his future as he leaves his village.

Key point

Biddy's virtues come to the fore here, as does the extent of the corruption of Pip's character. By the time he leaves the forge, Pip has begun to betray all those who genuinely care for him.

Q Why does Biddy criticise Pip so strongly?

Volume 2

This middle volume deals with Pip's life as a 'Gentleman' after he has inherited his fortune. Although he lives a quite secure, comfortable life, he achieves little apart from dwelling on his obsession with Estella. The volume ends abruptly as Magwitch confronts Pip with the shocking news that he is the source of Pip's fortune.

Chapter 1 (pp.163–71)

Summary: *Pip's first day in London.*

Pip meets Jaggers and his dour assistant, Wemmick, at Jaggers' office; he is treated to an impressive display of Jaggers' uncanny power over his clients. The beginning of Pip's new life is the opposite of what we might expect. London, rather than being the glittering prize that Pip had hoped for, is a squalid hellhole filled with 'filth and fat and blood and foam' (p.165). His first day in the city is spent among criminals in the gloomy shadow of Newgate Prison, an anticipation of the many traumas and disappointments that he will later experience.

Q What do we learn about Wemmick and Jaggers in this chapter?

Chapters 2–3 (pp.171–88)

Summary: *Pip moves into his new home and befriends Herbert.*

Pip is dismayed to find that his new London quarters are disgracefully unkempt. London, he begins to think, is 'decidedly overrated' (p.174). However, Pip's spirits brighten when he realises that he will be sharing his apartment with Herbert Pocket – coincidentally, the boy he defeated at Miss Havisham's. After Herbert coaches Pip on table manners and fills him in about Miss Havisham's sad past, the pair go to his family home to meet his negligent mother, nervous father (Miss Havisham's cousin), and younger brothers and sisters. Mrs Pocket's humorous neglect of her many children doubles as a serious comment on how children are treated appallingly by adults in this society.

Q What are your first impressions of Herbert?

Chapter 4 (pp.188–96)

Summary: *At the Pockets' house, Pip meets Drummle and Startop.*

The sinister Bentley Drummle and the foppish but pleasant Startop are introduced, both students staying at the Pockets' house. Pip spends time with Mrs Pocket (Herbert's mother) and her family; she continues to ignore her children's welfare. Mr Pocket, like Joe, is trapped in a failed marriage – another serious point delivered humorously. Dickens' frequent portrayals of unhappy marriages in this novel suggest his pessimistic view of the subject.

Chapters 5–6 (pp.196–210)

Summary: *Pip sees Jaggers at work, then dines at Wemmick's.*

Pip discusses his prospects with Mr Pocket (Herbert's father) and is befriended by Wemmick. After seeing Jaggers at work in court, Pip dines at Wemmick's pleasant mock-castle home, where he lives a cosy domestic life with his elderly father.

Key points

Jaggers is a respected lawyer, but his sordid line of work provides a stark contrast with earlier depictions of Joe's honest labour at the forge.

Wemmick's idyllic home life reveals that he is a bizarrely divided character: dry and repressed at work, but gentle and caring at home.

Q What do we learn about Jaggers from seeing him in court? What is Dickens suggesting about the legal profession?

Q How does Dickens convey the change in Wemmick's character between his home life and his work life?

Chapter 7 (pp.210–17)

Summary: *Dinner at Jaggers'.*

Pip dines at Jaggers' house with Drummle, Herbert and Startop. To Pip's confusion, Jaggers seems to be particularly interested in the odious Drummle. Drummle quickly becomes violent, and Jaggers intervenes to prevent him from assaulting the harmless Startop.

Q What does the dinner party scene tell us about Jaggers?

Chapter 8 (pp.217–25)

Summary: *Joe comes to London.*

Pip is called on in London by Joe, a meeting Pip would have preferred not to have. Joe soon leaves, conscious that Pip is acutely uncomfortable around him. This is the first time Pip realises that he may have hurt Joe, whose habit of calling him 'sir' symbolises how far the two have drifted apart. Joe, who tells Pip that they shouldn't meet anymore in London, retains a sense of warmth and dignity that contrasts with Pip's coldness.

Q Why does Pip say that he 'would have paid money' (p.218) to avoid seeing Joe?

Chapter 9 (pp.225–31)

Summary: *Pip meets the strange man from the Jolly Bargemen again.*

Leaving London for Miss Havisham's, Pip is forced to share a coach with two convicts; one of them is the man who gave him the two pounds at the Jolly Bargemen. Unrecognised, Pip overhears him saying that Magwitch has been transported to Australia for life. This chapter also shows the older narrator heavily criticising his younger self, admitting that he 'began to invent reasons and make excuses' in order to avoid Joe (p.225). When Pip reaches his village, he chooses to stay at the Blue Boar instead of the forge.

Q What excuses does the young Pip make to himself to justify avoiding Joe?

Chapter 10 (pp.231–44)

Summary: *Pip visits Miss Havisham.*

At Miss Havisham's house, Pip unexpectedly meets Orlick. He is now working for her as a doorman. When Pip sees Estella, who has grown into a young woman, his love is intensified. Estella tells Pip that she can never love him, then confronts Miss Havisham for making her incapable of this emotion. Delighted by Pip's distress, Miss Havisham urges him to maintain his doomed love for Estella. The scene is interrupted by the entrance of Jaggers. Pip dines with Estella, Jaggers and Sarah Pocket before leaving. For the first time, Pip sees the reality of a world without love. He finally realises that his infatuation is impossible and irrational – but by this stage, he can't help it.

Q Why does Miss Havisham urge Pip to fall in love with Estella?

Chapters 11–12 (pp.244–58)

Summary: *Back in London, Pip and Herbert see Wopsle in* Hamlet.

Pip returns to London without seeing Joe, but encounters his childhood nemesis, Trabb's boy, on the way. Herbert subtly attempts to discourage him from pursuing Estella, hinting that Jaggers may intend Pip and Estella to marry. Afterwards, the two go to see Wopsle in a comically inept performance of *Hamlet*.

Key point

This chapter contains some interesting parallels. Trabb's boy plays the servile role that Pip himself once played, while Pip can now afford to have a servant of his own. Pip's contempt for Trabb's boy underscores Dickens' message that most people will exploit others as soon as they get the chance.

Q Why does Herbert try to discourage Pip?

Q Why does Pip imagine himself playing 'Hamlet to Miss Havisham's ghost' (p.258)?

Chapters 13–14 (pp.258–71)

Summary: *Pip visits Newgate Prison, then dines with Estella.*

After Estella notifies him that she is coming to London, Pip meets Wemmick at Newgate Prison, where he is introduced to several of Wemmick and Jaggers' clients. Newgate Prison represents Pip's most literal connection with criminality. Pip is deeply disturbed by the experience (although he is in no danger), and feels utterly corrupted by his surroundings. As Pip virtually sees Estella as a divine being, he is unable to bear the thought of her finding out about his visit. During dinner, he again declares his love and is again rejected. After Estella confides in Pip about the suffering she has been subjected to by Miss Havisham, Pip drops her off at her new residence in Richmond and glumly heads home.

Q How does Pip feel after leaving the prison? Why?

Q Why does Pip pursue Estella if he is 'always miserable' around her (p.271)?

Chapters 15–16 (pp.272–85)

Summary: *Pip learns of his sister's death and returns to the forge.*

Pip and Herbert join a decadent club, and begin to squander their money. Their attempt to organise their finances is farcical because it is completely divorced from reality. Not having to earn a living has made Pip forget the importance of work. In a rare admission, Pip announces that he felt 'wonderful' when he learnt of his sister's death (p.278). A more sadistic side of Pip is appearing, and his bitter 'reunion' at the forge shows how contemptuous he has become. Pip insults Joe and Biddy by offering them money, which Biddy angrily rejects. By the time Pip returns to London, their friendship has frayed. Pip is in danger of becoming an unsympathetic character.

Q How is Pip's life affected by his newly acquired wealth?

Q Why does Biddy doubt that Pip will return?

Chapters 17–18 (pp.285–99)

Summary: *Pip comes of age, and financially assists Herbert.*

Confronting Pip over his spendthrift habits, Jaggers prepares to sign over Pip's entire inheritance. Pip tells Wemmick that he wishes to donate some of his money to Herbert anonymously, in order to support his friend's career.

Key point

Pip's action suggests that he understands Herbert's vulnerability and decides to protect him. In this respect, Pip is taking on the role of a benevolent father figure. This begins Pip's slow process of redemption by showing that he is capable of kindness.

Chapter 19 (pp.300–12)

Summary: *Pip sees Estella several times, and learns of her engagement. Estella confronts Miss Havisham.*

After Pip is again tormented by Estella, he realises that she 'was set to wreak Miss Havisham's revenge on men' (p.302) – a claim supported when Estella bitterly accuses Miss Havisham of destroying her soul with cruelty. Pip is devastated when he finds out that Estella and Drummle are soon to be married.

Key point

This is seemingly the end of Pip's ill-advised love story. After he learns of Estella's impending marriage, his life's purpose becomes unclear. The confrontation between Estella and Miss Havisham suggests, for the first time, that Estella is a complex character who is aware of her emotional shortcomings.

Chapter 20 (pp.312–24)

Summary: *Magwitch returns to Pip's house.*

A mysterious man visits Pip in his London apartment at night, revealing himself to be the convict that Pip helped on the marshes as a child. The horrified Pip, seeking to sever all ties with the convict, attempts to pay him back the two one-pound notes that he received as a gift years ago. Magwitch (going under the name 'Provis' in an attempt to escape police detection) tells Pip that he is responsible for Pip's fortune.

Key points

This pivotal chapter reveals that Pip has been mistaken about the source of his wealth all along. His utter revulsion derives from Magwitch's connection to the criminal world – to which Pip realises he is financially indebted.

Note the close parallels between Pip's treatment of Joe and his treatment of Magwitch. In both cases he shuns a father figure because he is ashamed of his background.

Q How does the return of Magwitch alter Pip's attitude towards his inheritance? Is this a logical reaction?

Volume 3

This volume charts the decline of Pip's fortunes after their peak in Volume 2. The first half concerns Pip's painful process of learning to accept Magwitch, while the second half concerns Magwitch's escape and its aftermath. By the end of this volume, the wounds Pip inflicted on his loved ones in Volumes 1 and 2 have been healed.

Chapter 1 (pp.327–40)

Summary: *Pip conceals Magwitch in his apartment.*

When Jaggers confirms that Magwitch is his benefactor, Pip's worst fears are confirmed. Although still stunned about the identity of his 'terrible patron' (p.334), Pip decides to protect Magwitch.

Q Why does Pip decide to assist Magwitch if he is repulsed by him?

Chapter 2 (pp.340–5)

Summary: *Pip and Herbert plot to smuggle Magwitch out of England.*

After Pip considers the illicit source of his wealth, and decides that the past few years of his life have been a mistake, he decides to quit his London life and return to the forge where he belongs. Together, Herbert and Pip plan to take Magwitch to safety by boat.

Key point

Pip's difficult decision to help Magwitch makes him a much more sympathetic character. The decision to return to the forge also marks the beginning of Pip's realisation that he has been unjust to Joe.

Q How does this episode deepen Pip and Herbert's friendship?

Chapter 3 (pp.346–53)

Summary: *Magwitch's life story.*

In Magwitch's flashback, he tells Pip of his harsh life, and how he was exploited and deceived by the criminal Compeyson. While he is speaking, Herbert reveals to Pip that Compeyson was Miss Havisham's unfaithful lover.

Q How does Magwitch's story make him into a more sympathetic character?

Chapter 4 (pp.353–8)

Summary: *Pip tries to see Estella, but meets Drummle on the way instead.*

While going to visit Estella at Richmond, Pip discovers that she has returned to Miss Havisham's. At the inn he meets Drummle again, who implies that he and Estella are engaged.

Q How is the rising aggression between Pip and Drummle conveyed in this scene?

Chapter 5 (pp.358–66)

Summary: *Pip sees Miss Havisham and Estella.*

Back at Miss Havisham's house, Pip accuses her of deceiving him about the true source of his money. While denying this, Miss Havisham agrees to pay for Herbert's tuition. Estella arrives and confirms that she is engaged to Drummle. At this news, Pip is devastated. Miss Havisham, realising the damage she has done to both Pip and Estella, feels remorse for the first time.

Key point

Just as Pip has been forced to come to terms with the consequences of his treatment of others, Miss Havisham is now also forced to confront the reality of the damage she has done to Pip and Estella's young lives. As with Pip's painful admission of guilt, Miss Havisham is humanised by her expression of remorse.

Chapter 6 (pp.366–73)

Summary: *Pip receives a written warning from Wemmick, and goes to his house to hide.*

Returning from Miss Havisham's, Pip finds a letter from Wemmick indicating that the police are after Magwitch. Pip goes to Wemmick's, and is told that Compeyson has returned to London.

Q Why does Wemmick risk his career to protect Magwitch?

Chapters 7–8 (pp.373–87)

Summary: *Pip walks to Clara's, where Magwitch is concealed; waiting for a sign from Wemmick, Pip attends another of Wopsle's disastrous performances.*

Pip goes to Herbert's girlfriend's lodging after learning that Magwitch has been hidden there. Pip and Herbert hatch a plan to smuggle him out of London by boat.

Key point

Herbert and Clara's idealised relationship offers the most positive vision of love in a world where so many relationships are less honourable.

Chapter 9 (pp.387–94)

Summary: *Pip dines at Jaggers' a second time.*

Pip dines with Wemmick and Jaggers at Jaggers' apartment, and finally realises that Jaggers' housekeeper is in fact Estella's mother. After dinner, Wemmick tells Pip the story of how Jaggers' housekeeper was accused of murdering another woman in a dispute over a man, how she had a child with this man, and how she stays with Jaggers in return for him successfully defending her from being convicted. This is the most important flashback in the narrative, providing crucial information about Estella's heritage and Jaggers' role in the story.

Q Does discovering Estella's heritage alter Pip's opinion of her? Why or why not?

Chapter 10 (pp.394–403)

Summary: *Pip revisits Miss Havisham for the last time, and she is badly burnt in a fire.*

When Pip returns to Satis House, he learns that Estella has permanently fled. Miss Havisham has realised the full consequences of her cruel actions and begs Pip for forgiveness. Pip has another vision of Miss Havisham's death. Shortly after this vision, there is a fire at the house in which both are burnt – Pip mildly, Miss Havisham severely. Miss Havisham will later die from her injuries.

Key point

In a sense, Pip will be 'freed' by the death of Miss Havisham, just as he was freed by the death of his sister, as it clears the way for him to regain a sense of normality in his life, and escape from the corrupt world into which he has fallen.

Q How are we encouraged to look at Miss Havisham differently in her final scene?

Chapters 11–12 (pp.404–15)

Summary: *Pip is nursed by Herbert, who tells Pip that Magwitch is Estella's father; Pip visits Jaggers, and tells him about Estella.*

Jaggers is stunned to hear Pip's news. He tells Pip how he saved Estella by entrusting her to Miss Havisham.

Key point

The revelation about Estella's parentage deepens the novel's theme of corruption: by being linked to Magwitch, Estella is shown to be just as embroiled in the criminal world as is Pip. As she is from a disadvantaged background, Pip's sense of class inferiority becomes meaningless.

Q Why does Jaggers take so much care not to seem surprised by Pip's news?

Chapter 13 (pp.416–21)

Summary: *Pip receives letters from Wemmick and Orlick.*

Pip recovers gradually from his injuries. As Pip and Herbert plan Magwitch's escape, Pip receives an anonymous letter telling him to meet the writer on the marshes, and duly returns there to meet him. Pip has not escaped the demons of his past; he is again pursued by monstrous forces beyond his control.

Q What is the significance of Pip's conversation with the landlord?

Chapter 14 (pp.421–34)

Summary: *Pip is nearly murdered at the kiln by Orlick.*

Orlick voices his resentment at Pip for thwarting his designs on Biddy, and admits to killing Pip's sister. Pip is saved at the last minute by Herbert, Startop and Trabb's boy, who follow him to the kiln. Orlick escapes into the night.

Key point

Trabb's boy's role in Pip's unexpected rescue again suggests that the novel's class antagonisms are slowly being overcome. Pip's eventual reconciliation with Joe completes this healing process.

Chapter 15 (pp.434–47)

Summary: *During the escape attempt, Compeyson is killed and Magwitch is captured.*

After being rescued, a feverish Pip is laid to rest in their flat. Waking the next morning, Pip, Herbert and Startop begin to execute Magwitch's escape. Travelling down the Thames on a boat with Magwitch, they are apprehended by the police, accompanied by Compeyson. After a struggle between the two, Compeyson is killed and Magwitch captured. Although the plan to free Magwitch fails, the journey can be seen as a success for Pip, whose role in Magwitch's daring escape attempt has completed his maturation process.

Q How has Magwitch's character, and Pip's attitude towards him, changed since his re-entry into Pip's life at the end of Volume 2?

Chapter 16 (pp.448–55)

Summary: *Pip loses his fortune, and Wemmick and Mrs Skiffins marry.*

Compeyson's death and Magwitch's imprisonment free Pip from the nightmare of his old life. The loss of Pip's fortune will allow him to reunite with his original family, whose virtues he has now learnt to appreciate.

Q How does Pip react to the loss of his fortune? Is this surprising?

Chapter 17 (pp.455–60)

Summary: *Magwitch is sentenced to death, but dies of natural causes before his execution.*

After Magwitch's trial, Pip goes to visit Magwitch in prison every day. His fear and loathing of the convict has finally truly vanished. Magwitch accepts that he is going to die. On his last visit, Pip tells the ailing Magwitch about his daughter, Estella. Immediately after hearing of her existence, Magwitch dies from his injuries.

Chapter 18 (pp.461–73)
Summary: *Pip falls into a fever and is nursed by Joe.*

Pip falls ill immediately after Magwitch's death, realising that he is now virtually alone in the world and impoverished. Herbert has gone to Egypt to fulfil the career that Pip has secretly created for him. Joe returns to London to nurse Pip back to health, then vanishes once Pip is fully recovered. Mulling over Joe's compassionate act, Pip decides to leave the city and return to the forge for good; he also resolves to marry Biddy.

Q Is Pip's decision to marry Biddy wise? Why or why not?

Chapter 19 (pp.473–81)
Summary: *Pip returns to his childhood home.*

Back in his village, Pip confronts Pumblechook for exploiting him. Although he had planned to propose to Biddy, he finds out that Biddy and Joe have just become married. Pip, chastened, asks for and receives Joe and Biddy's forgiveness.

Q Why does Pip wait for so long to confront Pumblechook?

Chapter 20 (pp.481–4)
Summary: *Pip returns to the village 11 years later.*

Pip returns to a much happier forge than he left; Biddy and Joe's son, a new Pip, now occupies the place by the hearth that used to be his. Returning to Miss Havisham's house, Pip finds Estella there. Although their meeting is subdued, it is implied that they will begin a relationship. The reunions at the end of the novel – between Pip and his family, and also between Pip and Estella – do not fall into the 'happily ever after' category. Joe's marriage to Biddy prevents Pip from marrying the 'right' woman, and his future with Estella is uncertain.

Q Does it seem plausible that Pip and Estella will live a happy life together?

CHARACTERS & RELATIONSHIPS

Pip Pirrip

Key quote

> 'I want to be a gentleman … I am not at all happy as I am. I am disgusted with my calling and with my life' (pp.127–8).

Pip, the novel's protagonist, is an anxious, brooding and flawed young man. Unlike most of Dickens' protagonists, Pip is not particularly sympathetic – in fact, much of the time he is quite unlikeable, as he is driven by an all-consuming sense of ambition that often causes him to neglect those who care for him.

Pip's life is dominated by an unrequited attachment to the beautiful Estella, which soon develops into an obsessive and persistent fixation, making it impossible for him to have a normal relationship. Pip's character is severely compromised when he inherits money, but we see his gradual and painful process of redemption from a selfish youth to a mature man who atones for his earlier mistreatment of others.

Parent figures

Parental relationships are one of the novel's major focuses. Often in the bildungsroman genre (see page 13 of this guide) an impressionable child is led by an experienced adult. This is replayed many times in *Great Expectations* with different results. Pip, who is essentially naive and unsure of which path to follow, is led in several different directions by a host of parent figures throughout his life. Most of these are unsuitable teachers, but a few of them are positive figures who offer him helpful guidance.

Pip and Magwitch

Key quote

> 'Yes, Pip, dear boy, I've made a gentleman on you! It's me wot has done it!' (p.319)

Magwitch, the convict Pip encounters in the opening scene, represents the dirt, poverty and criminality that Pip fears and despises: he is disgusted, for example, that Magwitch eats 'like [a] dog' (p.19). By providing Pip with the means for success, Magwitch – a bit like Dickens himself – stands in a godlike role to Pip's life. Behind the scenes, he orchestrates Pip's rise in society. Upon finally discovering the criminal source of his wealth, Pip is appalled; but his attitude towards Magwitch gradually changes, reflecting the changes taking place in his own character. Magwitch's revelation forces Pip to see him as a fellow human being rather than a disgusting object. To do this, Pip must learn to forget the snobbery that has allowed him to look down on those of lowly origins.

Magwitch, then, has an ambiguous role in Pip's life. On the one hand, his financial support of Pip is incredibly damaging. It causes Pip to abandon his 'true calling' as a blacksmith, and to take up useless pursuits instead. As Pip says after losing his money, 'I have been bred for no calling, and I am fit for nothing' (p.342). By robbing Pip of an occupation, Magwitch has effectively robbed Pip of a purpose. Yet Magwitch's influence is not entirely negative. By giving Pip the opportunity to leave his family home, he provides Pip with the chance to expand his world. Although Pip does not always like what he finds there, he returns to the forge with the knowledge that the lifestyle he originally desired is hollow and meaningless.

As Magwitch is figuratively a father to Pip, he is literally a father to Estella. Magwitch's rehabilitation from a despised convict to a cherished guardian by the time of his death depends on this fact for two reasons. First, it shows that Magwitch had an attachment to another person (Estella's mother) in the past; second, it makes Pip's love object more human by linking Estella to another person in Pip's life. The example of Magwitch teaches Pip to accept human imperfection – although this was certainly not Magwitch's intention. Firmly linking Pip's money to the sordid reality of crime, Magwitch deflates Pip's illusions about wealth and forces him to realise that its attainment does not entitle someone to avoid the rest of human society.

Pip and Compeyson

Key quote

> 'That evil genius, Compeyson, the worst of scoundrels among many scoundrels …' (p.407)

Compeyson is less a character than a living embodiment of Pip's worst fears. Although he rarely features in the narrative, Compeyson has a massive effect on those around him. This makes him one of the main drivers of the plot: by jilting Miss Havisham and leading the desperate Magwitch into a life of crime, he is thus indirectly responsible for the adoption of Estella, who was left in Miss Havisham's care after Magwitch's imprisonment. His 'livid' appearance (p.36) is the stuff of nightmares, and provides Pip with a powerful negative example. By operating as the 'bad convict' to Magwitch's 'good convict', he makes Magwitch's redemption from criminal to father figure more convincing.

Pip and Joe

Key quote

> 'Pip, dear old chap, life is made of ever so many partings welded together …' (p.224)

Joe is the most consistently benevolent of Pip's parent figures. With his 'simple dignity' and boundless compassion, Joe embodies all the qualities that Pip must learn if he is to reach his full human potential. Joe also represents one side of the division between moral and intellectual education. Conspicuously uncultured in his speech and manners, Joe lacks the resources to offer Pip the intellectual cultivation that he desires. The comical early scenes of Joe's attempts to read – which prompt Pip to remark that 'Joe's education, like Steam, was yet in its infancy' (p.46) – show his intellectual limitations. While Joe's moral guidance is not sufficient on its own to complete Pip's education, he enables a crucial part of Pip's personal growth.

Key point

Joe shines in the story by providing a quiet, steady example of exemplary conduct. He protects Pip from Mrs Joe as much as he can, yet avoids physically harming her because he remembers his father 'hammered away at my mother, most onmerciful' (p.46). Countering the examples of Estella and Miss Havisham – abused people who inflict abuse on others – Joe offers a positive solution to the cycles of violence that pervade *Great Expectations*.

The lessons taught by Joe about restraint, forbearance and loyalty are adopted by Pip at the end of the story. By selflessly caring for Pip during his illness, even after he has been rejected, Joe offers a model of pure friendship that is based on love rather than money or favours. At the conclusion, the fractured bond between Pip and Joe is restored, and Joe is rewarded with a happy marriage to Pip's childhood mentor, Biddy.

Pip and Mrs Joe

Key quote

'Who brought you up by hand?' (p.9)

Pip's aggressive elder sister is a stereotype of the harsh 19th-century parent. In this respect, she is the exact opposite of her husband, Joe. Her pin-filled 'impregnable bib' (p.8), which she never removes, is an apt symbol of her incapacity for physical intimacy and her curdled vision of human relationships. Mrs Joe can only communicate through violence, and her ongoing punishment of Pip goes some way towards explaining his ever-present sense of guilt over imagined crimes. Mrs Joe is similar to Miss Havisham in some ways, as both characters inflict pain on innocent people to compensate for the situation life has dealt them.

Mrs Joe, then, provides another negative role model for Pip, her behaviour representing everything that must be avoided. Her unpleasantness also helps to solidify the bond between Pip and Joe, which remains firm even after years of neglect by Pip. Mrs Joe's relationship with Pip improves after she has been physically incapacitated, and therefore incapable of violence. Left mute after her attack, she asks for forgiveness from Joe and Pip shortly before her death. Most importantly, though, her model of parenting is made obsolete by the far more benevolent example of Joe and Biddy's marriage.

Pip and Pumblechook

Key quote

'... this is him as I ever sported with in his days of happy infancy!' (p.475)

Pumblechook's rank opportunism teaches Pip about the difference between genuine and feigned emotion. Before Pip becomes rich, Pumblechook supports Mrs Joe's abuse of the boy. When he learns of Pip's wealth, this changes, and Pumblechook tries to style himself as Pip's benefactor. The antithesis of the altruistic Joe (Pip's real benefactor), Pumblechook is another failed parent figure. He illustrates the deceptive potential of manners, showing that external politeness has nothing to do with internal virtue.

Pip and Miss Havisham

Key quote

'Love her, love her, love her!' (p.243)

Pip and Miss Havisham have a complex and frequently changing relationship. She begins as his mentor, yet he ends as hers. Although her advice to Pip seems positive at times, as she clearly feels affection for him, she is ultimately another failed parent figure.

Miss Havisham initiates Pip's journey in the wrong direction by introducing the spectre of money into his simple, secluded world. Pip's sense of ambition is formed after he gains the impression that obtaining wealth and power will enable him to win Estella's hand. Pip does not realise at the time that Miss Havisham's personality has been distorted by bitterness. Only later does he understand that 'in shutting out the light of day, she had shut out infinitely more' (p.399). By then it is too late.

Although the lessons that Miss Havisham tries to teach Pip are disastrously misguided, the grief she causes him enables his human qualities to emerge. When he finally understands that Miss Havisham has made Estella into an inhuman, unfeeling person, Pip frustrates Miss Havisham's plan by offering Estella forgiveness – a compassionate gesture that leaves Miss Havisham in 'a ghastly stare of pity and remorse' (p.365).

Key point

Miss Havisham begins by trying to destroy the lives of others, and ends up being forced by Pip to confront the effects of her sadistic behaviour. Like Mrs Joe, she is humanised by her trauma, and her character is redeemed when she apologises for the unnecessary pain she has caused.

Pip and Jaggers

Key quote

'Everybody should know his own business.' (p.409)

The relationship between Pip and Jaggers resembles that of a distant parent to a child. Jaggers possesses both major strengths and severe weaknesses. Unlike many other figures of authority in the story, Jaggers never intends to deceive Pip; but he is an extremely limited person who has had to crush all spontaneous feeling within himself in order to retain his composure in his difficult job. As a consequence of his repression, he looks at the world with an intensely 'guarded and suspicious' manner that makes him seem less human in Pip's eyes (p.292).

Love interests

There are two competing love interests in Pip's life, both of which are unsuccessful, though in different ways.

Pip and Biddy

Key quote

'If I could only get myself to fall in love with you!' (p.131)

Pip's childhood tutor, the intelligent and caring Biddy, has a deep and lasting affection for Pip. She represents what might have been possible if

Pip had not fallen for Estella. In many ways, Biddy represents Dickens' stereotypical view of women as either purely angelic beings or purely evil, but rarely anything in between. Although Pip tells Biddy that she would make a good wife, his obsession with Estella prevents their union. Logically, Biddy is the 'right choice' for Pip, and he comes to recognise this. His inability to marry Biddy in the end highlights the difference between *Great Expectations* and a more conventional novel of development: its recognition that humans do not always act logically or admirably, and that things do not always turn out the way they are supposed to in fairytales.

Biddy also helps Pip's development by serving as the voice of his conscience. Few people stand up to Pip after he has gained his fortune, but Biddy always lets him know when he has done wrong – for example, when he falsely pretends that he will come back to visit Joe. Although Pip indignantly tells her that her behaviour demonstrates 'a very bad side of human nature' (p.284), his older self admits that 'Biddy was quite right' (p.285).

Pip and Estella

Key quote

'I am what you have made me.' (p.304)

Estella fuels Pip's wish to 'do all the shining deeds of the young Knight of romance, and marry the Princess' (p.231). It takes many years for Pip to understand that Estella does not live up to this fairytale ideal. Cold, beautiful and compelling, Estella is another child who has been treated harshly by adults. Estella's upbringing destroys her capacity for love, and Miss Havisham's savage efforts to 'train' her leave her emotionally cold – or even sadistic – towards others. Despite this, Pip falls in love with her at first sight and remains in love with her throughout his life. His unsuitable choice of role model (Miss Havisham) is coupled with an unsuitable choice of lover.

Unlike some other relationships in the novel, the one between Estella and Pip remains virtually static because Estella lacks the capacity for growth. Like Miss Havisham, she is trapped in her past. Their prolonged and futile courtship ritual eventually teaches Pip about the dangers of allowing fantasy to overshadow reality. Although Pip is spurred on by visions of greatness for most of his young life, the mundane reality of Estella's shattered personality teaches him to relinquish his unachievable dreams in favour of something more realistic and concrete.

Unfortunately, the bleak message about the danger of delusions is watered down by the novel's revised final chapter, which unconvincingly hints at a final reconciliation between Pip and Estella, perhaps even offering the hope of a love affair. Pip's ambiguous last line – 'I saw the shadow of no parting from her' (p.484) – does suggest that the two may be able to be happy together, but our knowledge of Estella makes this seem unlikely. The novel's original ending is far more faithful to its sober message about the dangers of unrealistic expectations. In this ending, Pip meets Estella one final time before being separated from her forever. This conclusion contains the more profound message that the possibility of being happy with Estella was always a figment of Pip's imagination.

Friends

There are several characters who could be considered Pip's 'friends' in the novel, but we will look at the two most important ones.

Pip and Wemmick

Key quote

'This is altogether a Walworth sentiment.' (p.455)

Wemmick offers an interesting counterpoint to Jaggers. Like him, Wemmick is offhand, even brutal, to his clients. Unlike Jaggers, however, Wemmick is able to lead a relatively normal life outside of work. He does this by separating his professional and private lives (see 'Repression' in Themes, Ideas and Values).The most important lesson that Wemmick teaches Pip regards caring for others. The care that Wemmick lavishes on his Aged Parent contrasts starkly with the lack of care Pip bestows on Joe. By witnessing the lengths to which Wemmick goes to make his father comfortable in his later life, Pip is reminded of the importance of fulfilling family obligations.

Pip and Herbert

Key quote

'"Now, Handel," Herbert replied, in his gay, hopeful way, "it seems to me that in the despondency of the tender passion, we are looking into our gift-horse's mouth with a magnifying-glass."' (p.249)

The book's least complex and most genial character, Herbert brings out the best in Pip. In his only unambiguously good deed, Pip anonymously funds Herbert's rise to a partnership in his firm, even going to the trouble of asking Miss Havisham to continue the payments after he loses his money. The friendship between Pip and Herbert is a benevolent reflection of the exploitative friendships in the novel. Most importantly, Pip's anonymous financial support of Herbert is a mirror image of Magwitch's anonymous financial support of Pip. There are many similarities, yet Pip's treatment of Herbert is far more positive than Magwitch's treatment of Pip.

Why is Pip's support of Herbert admirable, while Magwitch's support of Pip is exploitative? Unlike Magwitch, Pip does not use his patronage to 'own' Herbert. Instead, he establishes Herbert's career purely out of the goodness of his heart, delighted that 'my expectations had done some good to somebody' (p.299). From Herbert, Pip learns the benefits of unconditional friendship, and their steady, respectful relationship anchors Pip when he is in danger of losing his bearings.

Enemies

Two characters in particular can be seen as Pip's enemies. It has been suggested that both can be seen as 'evil' versions of Pip, who carry out his secret desires of revenge against those who have wronged him (Moynahan 1999, p.661).

Pip and Drummle

Key quote

'*Oh*, Lord!' (p.215)

Drummle is everything that Pip threatens to become – a villainous, depraved, boorish aristocrat. The source of Drummle's deep and inexhaustible hatred of others is unclear. And yet in some ways he is a sort of idol to Pip: he is rich, undeniably aristocratic and supremely comfortable with wielding power over others. These are qualities that Pip does not possess, but often wishes he did.

Pip and Orlick

Key quote

> 'You was favoured, and he was bullied and beat.' (p.426)

Initially Joe Gargery's assistant at the forge, Orlick develops a hostile attitude towards Pip. Orlick's violent acts during the novel, especially his battery of Pip's sister and later of Pumblechook, do suggest that he is carrying out Pip's unconscious bidding. Like Drummle, Orlick offers Pip a vision of what to avoid. His insistent, underhand pursuit of Biddy disgusts Pip and makes him more protective of her than he otherwise might have been. Orlick can also be seen to represent Pip's fear of the working class. Explicitly part of the world of the forge rather than the city, Orlick embodies all Pip's fears about the dirty, dangerous and threatening working classes.

THEMES, IDEAS & VALUES

Class and money

The plot of *Great Expectations* revolves around the interrelated issues of class and money. Almost every character is affected by the never-ending quest for wealth, and almost all those in the 'lower classes' struggle ferociously to 'move up' to a more respectable class. Although Dickens sympathises with this impulse to an extent, he shows how many people's pursuit of wealth and class status comes at the expense of more important things.

Greed and ambition

As someone who strives to raise himself financially and socially, Pip perfectly illustrates the potentially corrosive effects of this type of ambition. His positive qualities gradually become corrupted by his pursuit of wealth, and he betrays those who love him. The trappings of an aristocratic lifestyle have a destructive effect on Pip's ability to understand what is important in life. As Pip ascends the class scale, he gains several 'false friends' – most notably Pumblechook, who flatters him, just as Miss Havisham's relatives, who lust after her inheritance, flatter her. The grovelling attitude of these characters suggests that wealth is incompatible with friendship. Crucially, one character who is unaffected by the spell of money is Joe. He may call Pip 'sir', but he has no designs on Pip's wealth. He quietly criticises Pip for letting the money go to his head, saying, 'You and me is not two figures to be together in London' (p.224).

Corruption, criminality and poverty

The story strongly condemns many aspects of modern urban life, which Dickens represents as corrupt in comparison to the simpler rural environment. London, while interesting, is a negative place, its defining symbol being Newgate Prison. By closing Pip's story in the countryside rather than in the city, Dickens suggests that people must escape the corruption of the modern city in order to function normally.

The taint of criminality in the novel is inescapable. Jaggers tries to rid himself of it by compulsively 'washing his hands with his scented soap' (p.210). Similarly, Pip tries to cleanse himself of his connection with Magwitch by paying back 'two fat sweltering one-pound notes' (p.78) with two 'clean and new' ones (p.318). Dickens' early novels contained many figures of pure evil who murdered or stole just for the fun of it, such as Fagin from *Oliver Twist*, but his views became more complex by the end of his career. In *Great Expectations* he offers a contrast between the 'good' criminal, Magwitch, a 'ragged little creetur' forced into a life of crime (p.346), and the 'bad' criminal, Compeyson, who 'was a dab at the ways of gentlefolks' (p.347). Magwitch is a fundamentally decent person who became a criminal only in order to feed himself; Compeyson's criminality stems from his inner evil.

'New money' and the middle class

Just as *Great Expectations* is suspicious of the aristocracy, it is also suspicious of the middle-class financial occupations that were emerging around that time. Herbert Pocket, who aims to become an accountant, is a good example. When asked by Pip what he does for a living, he replies vaguely that 'you look about you' (p.184). In contrast, Joe the blacksmith represents hardworking honesty, and Pip's decision to sacrifice this career for an idle life of leisure is condemned by Dickens. Before Pip meets Estella, he sees the forge as 'the glowing road to manhood and independence' (p.107); yet afterwards, he sees physical labour as 'coarse and common' (p.107). The rest of his life story makes it clear that his original attitude was the correct one.

Morality

Pip is obsessively concerned with the morality of his actions, yet his dilemmas take place against a wider backdrop of injustice and immorality infecting the whole of society. The all-pervasive reach of the law in the novel, coupled with the suggestion that it can be manipulated by unscrupulous people, suggests that *Great Expectations*' world has undergone a serious moral breakdown.

Innocence versus experience

The novel is structured around these two opposites. Innocence is represented by the young Pip, who is often unaware of the harm he causes to others; experience is represented by the mature Pip, who frequently looks back on his earlier life with regret. Pip's journey from innocence to experience is painful. While he yearns to become an experienced adult so that he can win Estella's hand, he cannot shake off his immature desire for perfect love until it is far too late. Dickens recognises the appeal of this impossible ideal, yet he also suggests that losing our youthful illusions is necessary in order to enter the adult world.

Guilt and revenge

Pip is haunted by a fear of persecution out of proportion to any crime he has committed. This originates when he steals from his sister to help Magwitch, but it continues long after. Julian Moynahan notes that Pip's assumption of his own guilt 'does not seem to correspond with any real criminal acts or intentions' (Moynahan 1999, p.655). A clue lies in Pip's underlying desire to punish those he dislikes. Moynahan suggests that all those who are punished in the novel 'have hurt, humiliated, or thwarted Pip in some important way' (Moynahan 1999, p.660). Because these people are punished in accordance with Pip's wishes, Pip 'experiences the equivalent of a murderer's guilt' (Moynahan 1999, p.662).

Q Do you think this is an accurate assessment of Pip's feelings of guilt?

Injustice

Pip tells us that 'in the little world in which children have their existence whosoever brings them up, there is nothing so finely perceived and so finely felt, as injustice' (p.63). Yet the novel has an ambiguous attitude towards justice. While the stern Jaggers goes some way in representing the law as it is supposed to be – impartial and objective – the novel suggests that the legal system is unable to deliver justice to the bulk of the population. Injustice, Dickens implies, is the natural state of the world. Many characters in the novel are denied justice because they are poor.

The unequal availability of education for rich and poor leads to long-term lack of opportunity, and abused children such as Magwitch often lead disastrous adult lives. Those lucky enough to receive a just outcome are in the minority.

At Magwitch's trial, 'two-and-thirty men and women' are tried at the same time (p.457), and all are condemned. Pip's observation of 'a broad shaft of light between the two-and-thirty and the judge, linking both together' (p.458) suggests that the court's rushed 'guilty' verdict is unjust because it denies their shared humanity. Still, it is important to remember that Dickens supports the idea that genuine justice is achievable. The novel itself can be seen as a kind of trial: though it puts good people through many hardships, the good are rewarded and the bad punished by the end. In its commitment to the idea that morally virtuous people will eventually thrive, *Great Expectations* is a highly optimistic book.

Loyalty

Dickens' characters are quite neatly divided between those who are loyal towards others and those who are not. Magwitch is the most prominent symbol of loyalty, as he honours his promise to Pip all his life. Joe, of course, is unfailingly loyal to Pip, and Wemmick protects Pip even at the risk of breaking the law. The violation of loyalty forms a larger part of *Great Expectations*. Although Pip feels 'free' after breaking his bond with Joe – symbolised by the burning of his indentures (p.146) – his freedom is an illusion because it is based on an act of disloyalty. In time, Pip realises the harmful effects of his choice to break his ties with Joe, who forgives him for this disloyal act.

Relationships

The novel is filled with exploitative relationships between people who seek to take advantage of others. There are some major exceptions – Joe's relationship with Pip, and Pip's relationship with Herbert, for example – which stand out because they are so unusual. As in so many other areas, money is the main cause of relationship failure.

Exploitative relationships

Power is the other main cause of inequality in relationships, the most obvious case being the relationship between Pip and Magwitch. Magwitch, who provides Pip with the funds to become a gentleman, actually considers Pip to be his property. While he is grateful to Pip for his good deed, he treats him as if he were a kind of zoo animal, looking with great amusement at Pip's clothing and furniture. Boasting that he 'owns a brought-up London gentleman' (p.321), Magwitch compromises his financial generosity towards Pip with this conviction that he possesses him. Estella is in a parallel situation, as Miss Havisham protects and nurtures her only as a means of gaining revenge.

Dominating relationships become the norm, as those who are exploited usually go on to exploit others. Just as Compeyson tries to dominate Magwitch by exploiting his poverty and ignorance, Magwitch dominates Pip in a similar way. Pip, in turn, dominates the Avenger, the servant whom he hires to do his odd jobs. This pattern is visible elsewhere. If Miss Havisham dominates Estella, Estella then dominates Pip by taunting him. Drummle dominates Estella inside their marriage by forcing her to do his bidding. Mrs Joe 'owns' the young Pip, treating him more as a possession than as a human being. Jaggers 'owns' Molly (Estella's mother), keeping her as a maid in his house.

In a telling metaphor, Pip compares his situation as Magwitch's protégé with that of Dr Frankenstein, 'pursued by the misshapen creature he had impiously made' (p.339). This is a revealing comparison, as Pip could just as easily be seen as the monster who has been 'created' by Magwitch.

Key point

The suggestion is that unequal relationships dehumanise both people, as they are based on principles of convenience rather than on those of true friendship.

Of course Dickens does not suggest that all relationships are intrinsically exploitative, a point illustrated by Pip's relationship with Herbert. Just as Magwitch anonymously donates a fortune to Pip, Pip anonymously sets up Herbert in a career. The crucial difference is that Pip does not help Herbert in order to control him.

Obsessive and irrational relationships

Dickens is essentially a romantic whose work repeatedly evokes the healing power of love. *Great Expectations* represents a significant departure from these conventional, positive ideas of love, and acknowledges how this feeling can easily become distorted by lust or obsession. There are many such relationships in the novel. For example, Orlick's pursuit of Biddy is seen primarily in threatening, sexual terms, and Drummle's courting of Estella is also seen negatively.

Most importantly, unlike in a traditional romance, the 'right' people do not always end up together as we expect them to. When Pip tells Biddy, 'If I could only get myself to fall in love with you!' (p.131), he signals his acknowledgement that Biddy would have been the more sensible choice of partner, while admitting that his obsession with Estella makes this impossible. Pip must learn to accept the idea of compromise to reach maturity. Later in the novel, he intends to ask Biddy to 'go through the world' with him (p.472), demonstrating that he has learnt many lessons from his failed attempt to achieve the perfect romance with Estella, but by this time it is too late.

There are a few relationships based on respect between compatible partners: Joe and Biddy; Wemmick and Miss Skiffins; and Herbert and Clara. By making virtually all other partnerships in the novel deeply flawed, Dickens recognises that people seldom act rationally when falling in love, and they often do so for selfish or non-admirable reasons.

Relationships within the family

'Hearth scenes' frequently feature in Dickens, and many of his works, such as *Oliver Twist,* end when the hero creates an ideal nuclear family. In Dickens' early work, people are generally happy when they are within a caring family circle, and unhappy when they are outside it. *Great Expectations,* however, suggests that the family hearth presents a perfect environment for misery, as the book contains many more unhappy families than happy ones. Pip's initial family is deeply dysfunctional, with the bond between Pip and Joe crushed at every opportunity by Pip's rampaging sister. Another 'family' featured is that of Miss Havisham and Estella, which proves an ideal breeding ground for cruelty. The privacy offered by the family, which is often valued in Dickens' earlier work, becomes a potential threat in *Great Expectations*.

However, while Dickens is pessimistic about the prospects of many families, he is not criticising the idea of the family itself. As in his other works, Dickens supports the idea that a properly functioning family holds the best possibility of providing happiness and fulfilment. The failures of the various families in the story become even more glaring when contrasted with the success of the 'perfect family' created at the novel's conclusion – that of Biddy, Joe and their children (p.481). This idealised family is an inversion of the dysfunctional family triangle of Pip, Joe and Mrs Joe.

Psychological states

Several extreme psychological states are explored in *Great Expectations*, more than in Dickens' other novels. Many of the characters are psychotic, repressed, severely depressed or violent. Just as Dickens connects criminality and poverty to social failure, he connects mental illness to unhealthy social pressures.

Madness and eccentricity

By making so many of his characters eccentrics, Dickens suggests that insanity has become normal in this society. And even when characters are not mad, they are usually maladjusted in some way – many of Dickens' characters are defined by bizarre tics and habits that suggest compulsive personalities. For example, Jaggers is defined by his biting and thrusting of his 'great forefinger' (p.133); Mr Pocket by his efforts to lift himself up by his hair (p.192); Wemmick by his post-office mouth (p.172); Magwitch by the 'click' in his throat when he eats (p.320); Drummle by his repetition of the phrase, '*Oh*, Lord!' (p.215). Most of these strange habits are presented as a product of external pressures –

for example, Jaggers' obsessive-compulsive behaviour suggests that he is displacing the effects that his occupation (which forces him to associate with criminals) has on his sense of right and wrong.

Repression

In comparison to today, early 19th-century England was an extremely formal and repressed environment in which people were discouraged from showing emotion in public. The character of Wemmick is the clearest illustration of how people deal with having to hide their true feelings behind a professional facade. The 'real' Wemmick is only on display outside of work hours. Wemmick's house, outside of London, is a place in which he is able to freely express his natural kindness and ingenuity. The pressure of concealing these aspects from public view makes him seem robotic in public, a quality encapsulated by his compressed 'post-office' mouth. Wemmick copes, in other words, by developing a split personality. Jaggers is astonished when he finds out about Wemmick's private life, asking in disbelief, '*You* with a pleasant home?' (p.412). Wemmick has managed, in other words, to conceal his real self from his employer for years.

Key point

Wemmick copes by separating himself into two parts, but others don't cope as well. Miss Havisham is the clearest example of the damage done by repressing natural human feelings – by halting her life at the moment of her humiliation, she becomes a kind of living tomb to her emotions.

Self-deception

The novel's pessimistic attitude towards humanity is summed up in many of the characters' capacity for self-deception. This recurrent theme is most completely explored in the character of Pip, whose greed has destroyed his ability to see the truth about himself and others. As narrator, from his wiser perspective, Pip recognises this youthful folly: 'That I should innocently take a bad half-crown of somebody else's manufacture, is reasonable enough; but that I should knowingly reckon the spurious coin of my own make as good money!' (p.225). Of course, Pip's entire life story is only made possible by self-deception. He deceives himself about Estella, about Miss Havisham's patronage, and about his own happiness. When he finally learns to appraise his life honestly, he realises that the period of his 'expectations' has been an intensely unhappy one.

Social issues

Representations of femininity

Although many of Dickens' characters are extraordinary inventions, his imagination tended to fail when creating women, whom he most often represented as 'angelic' beings lacking the complex characteristics found in real people. While *Great Expectations* improves on this by representing some female characters as fully rounded beings, the novel still deals in the stereotyped idea of women that Dickens returned to throughout his career. Pip's choice between Biddy and Estella is typical of Dickens, as it is a version of the plot in which a man is torn between the 'good' and the 'bad' woman. The two poles of the female stereotype can be seen in Biddy – a nurturing, pure figure – and Estella – a cruel, sexually powerful figure.

Estella, an extremely limited character, is at least given a coherent history: she is sympathetic, despite her unfeeling nature, because she has been deprived of love all her life. While Estella fits the 'evil woman' stereotype in some respects, the reader's knowledge of her brutal past makes her seem damaged rather than evil. As she says to Miss Havisham, 'I must be taken as I have been made' (p.306). Although Biddy – pure-hearted, timid and kind – is essentially the opposite of Estella, she is not as one-dimensional as she first seems. She has the presence of mind to criticise Pip for his cruel treatment of Joe, asking him, 'Have you never considered that he may be proud?' (p.149).

Miss Havisham straddles the extremes of purity and evil. Her abuse of Estella and her callous manipulation of Pip are obviously malign, yet they spring from the damage that Compeyson's ill use has inflicted on her. She is symbolically a virgin, having been deserted on her wedding day: the decaying cake and bridal dress are powerful symbols of withered female sexuality. However, she is humanised at the end of the novel when she repents for the treatment she has inflicted on Estella and apologises to Pip for her exploitation of his love for Estella.

Representations of masculinity

Dickens is also concerned about the role of males in society. He offers several versions of masculinity, most of which are defective in some way. In some characters (such as Drummle and Orlick) masculinity lapses into brutality. Others (such as Startop) are insufficiently masculine. The fact that there are so many dysfunctional or inadequate males in the novel suggests that Dickens holds the view that there is something fundamentally wrong with how society views men. Pip's society's strenuous efforts to suppress the natural expression of male sexuality and affection has led to something much darker – a society of men who can only express their emotions in aggressive or deviant ways, or else shut out their emotions altogether.

Society's repression of the nurturing side of males, Dickens suggests, creates brutes like Drummle, or (at best) imposing and unfriendly people like Jaggers. Fortunately, Dickens does offer a way out of this worrying situation by including *positive* male figures – most notably Joe, but also eventually Pip himself – who are able to combine masculine strength with emotional openness.

Child abuse and neglect

Biddy and Joe's young children at the novel's conclusion can look forward to a childhood of love and care. The rest of the children in *Great Expectations* are not so lucky. The mass of neglected children in this novel continues one of Dickens' major concerns – the abuse and neglect of children in Victorian England. The episode with Mrs Pocket, in which she reads her novel while 'forgetting all about the baby on her lap' (p.193), suggests that adults do not always have children's best interests at heart.

Pip himself is the clearest example of an abused child, but there are many others. Almost every life story we hear of in the book is a sad and violent one. Estella is abandoned and raised by a sadistic step-parent;

Magwitch is orphaned and cast off in the world until falling into a life of vice and criminality, growing up 'thieving turnips' to survive (p.346); Joe is raised by an alcoholic father who was 'given to drink' and regularly 'hammered away' at him and his mother (p.46).

Although to some extent Great Expectations implies that abused children become abusive adults, its depiction of Joe – the one character who avoids repeating his traumatic past – suggests that the cycle of abuse can be broken. At the end, Pip spends time with Joe and Biddy's child, reassuring us that he 'did *not* rumple his hair' (p.481). With this compassionate gesture, Pip creates a sense of hope that the horrors inflicted on children in the story have been overcome.

DIFFERENT INTERPRETATIONS

Different interpretations arise from different responses to a text. Over time, a text will evoke a wide range of responses from its readers, who may come from various social or cultural groups and live in very different places and historical periods. Responses by critics and reviewers can be published in newspapers, journals and books, both online and in print. They can also be expressed in discussions among readers in the media, classrooms, book groups and so on. While there is no single correct reading or interpretation of a text, it is important to understand that an interpretation is more than an 'opinion' – it is the justification of a point of view on the text. To present an interpretation of the text based on your point of view you must use a logical argument and support it with relevant evidence from the text.

The critics' viewpoints

Great Expectations is one of the most frequently analysed texts in the history of literature. As such, it has been interpreted in many different ways by many different critics in the century and a half since its publication. The following is an attempt to summarise some of the most influential approaches to the text; however, this summary is only a small cross-section of the field.

Contemporary interpretations

Literary criticism in the 19th century was substantially narrower than it is today, when many different approaches are possible. Several contemporary reviewers condemned *Great Expectations* for its implausibility, a fact that illustrates how much our expectations of fiction have changed. It would not make sense to criticise the book for its lack of realism today, since its fantasy aspects are clearly intentional; however, the *Dublin University Magazine*, for example, viewed these as 'utterly absurd' (*Great Expectations: Norton Critical Edition,* p.622). Another contemporary reviewer attacked the book for its physical inconsistencies, pointing out that Miss Havisham's wedding dress 'had only grown yellow and faded' in 25 years of use (*Great Expectations: Norton Critical Edition,* p.626). Some critics had more subtle concerns: a more perceptive contemporary critic rebuked Dickens for 'giving us so few characters and so many caricatures' (*Great Expectations: Norton Critical Edition,* p.624).

Marxist/class-based interpretations

As discussed, the classic plot of advancement, in which the poor hero casts off his humble origins in order to gain his fortune, provides the bare bones for Dickens' novel. The novel's comments about class conflict can be considered Marxist because they are based on an idea that would not have been alien to Marx: that the rich refuse to acknowledge their utter dependence on the labour of the poor. By enjoying his inherited riches while avoiding physical labour, Pip indulges in the fantasy that money magically appears from above, rather than having to be generated by those below.

Class-based interpretations of *Great Expectations* differ in several respects, but they generally agree that the novel draws attention to a 'hideous underworld of labour' (House 1999, p.645). Pip feels intense shame about his humble origins, but crossing through class boundaries merely gives him access to a world that is morally and spiritually worse than the poorer one he has left. At its simplest, the novel suggests that 'violence and brutality ... also exist in the supposedly refined society of London' (Gilmour 1999, p.582).

While different critics point out different implications of Pip's upward journey across class barriers, all agree that the novel critiques the injustice of the moneyed classes' dependence on – and failure to acknowledge – the working class. In this sense, the novel can be seen as anti-capitalist. Although Dickens did not have revolutionary tendencies, *Great Expectations* clearly addresses the injustices built into the class system.

Psychoanalytic interpretations

Because *Great Expectations'* protagonist has such a complex mental life, the novel has been interpreted psychoanalytically by several critics. Pip often experiences psychologically extreme states, including visions and hallucinations. Although these can seem random and inconsequential, they begin to make more sense when interpreted in terms of Pip's inner, or unconscious, desires. Psychoanalytic readings claim that there is a buried plot beneath *Great Expectations'* obvious surface plot of the boy who wishes to become successful and ends up finding out that love is more important than money. The buried plot is darker than the surface one because it is about Pip's *repressed* emotions – that is, all the feelings that he cannot express in his society.

There are two major groups of psychoanalytic readings. The first sees the novel's buried plot as one of repressed violence. Pip is quite shy, but he often becomes very angry with others. Sometimes he even imagines that they are killed or injured. These imaginings make sense, according to psychoanalysis, if Pip actually *wants* the things in his dreams and fantasies to occur. All the people who Pip imagines in pain are those who have wronged him. His buried (or repressed) desire to punish those who get in his way comes true when these people – for example, Mrs Joe, Miss Havisham and Drummle – are hurt or killed in the course of the novel.

Two psychoanalytic readings, by Peter Brooks and Michael Ginsburg, centre on the ambiguous figure of Miss Havisham. While she represents, for Pip, 'the world of fairy tales and fantasy', she is also 'the witch who holds in her castle … the imprisoned princess' (Ginsburg 1999, p.699). Brooks agrees, casting Miss Havisham as 'the Fairy Godmother' who also represents 'craziness and morbidity' (Brooks 1999, p.682). The surface version of Pip's life, in which Miss Havisham is his fairytale benefactor, masks the repressed plot in which she is an evil presence.

Feminist interpretations

As the novel's most memorable female figure, Miss Havisham has gained her share of critical attention. This once-vivacious woman has chosen to entomb herself in her mansion. Why does she do this? While Dickens often seems to paint Miss Havisham as vicious, several feminist critics have noticed that she is made this way by the patriarchal system that exploited her, becoming mentally unstable only after being spurned by a man. Linda Raphael, for instance, claims that Miss Havisham's confinement 'repeats the fate of many Victorian women' (Raphael 1999, p.706): after she 'fails to understand the system that works against her', she 'seeks to revenge herself against society on its own terms' (Raphael 1999, p.709).

This interpretation sees Dickens using Miss Havisham to raise the issue of the mistreatment of women in marriage – a fate that is raised again with Estella after she marries the abusive Drummle. While Miss Havisham is not a particularly sympathetic figure, this interpretation of her character suggests that she gives voice to the suffering of women in Victorian society at the hands of unscrupulous men. Although Dickens plainly criticises how marriage effectively made women into the property of men, it is important to remember that he does not reject the idea of patriarchy altogether. This is clear in his fundamental support of the institution of marriage: while recognising that bad marriages exploit women, he is equally confident that good marriages are possible; in them, women are given the opportunity to be happy. *Great Expectations*, then, attacks bad marriages, not marriage in general.

Two interpretations

1. *Great Expectations* is an inspirational story about a boy escaping from the trap of poverty and climbing the social ladder against the odds.
2. *Great Expectations* is a story about the emptiness of wealth and the pointlessness of success.

Interpretation 1

This interpretation sees Pip's escape from the forge as, on balance, a good thing. Although he suffers many hardships while he is in London, and the life that he had hoped for is not as wonderful as he had imagined, it is obvious that Pip gains the opportunity to grow as a person and have interesting experiences by finding out about the world – opportunities that he never would have had back at the forge.

Joe the blacksmith is such an appealing character that his limitations are easy to forget. But although he cares deeply for Pip, he is unable to provide Pip with the intellectual and cultural stimulation for which he yearns. Even Wopsle's embarrassing theatre performances in London allow him to branch out from the stagnant provincial life of the marshes. The nostalgic tone with which Dickens describes the forge is appealing, but it is difficult not to empathise with the young Pip's wish to become a gentleman. The world that he inhabits at the story's beginning is cruel, stunted and backward. He has nobody with whom to share his interests, and his future prospects are bleak.

Dickens' characterisation of London is often misunderstood, because of its significant flavour of criminality. However, Newgate Prison is only a small part of Pip's varied experiences there. He is able to improve indisputably his material comfort in his new life: although the clothing made for him by the tailor is looked at suspiciously by the simple people from his village, it allows Pip to present himself as a respectable person, something that he was not able to do before. Pip's hiring of a servant is another measure of his success. He is able to live a life of substantial comfort and luxury for a considerable time. Pip's efforts to support Herbert Pocket financially make nonsense of the idea that he has been corrupted by his wealth. However, he does use his wealth to strike back at those who tormented him when he was a child.

Although Pip returns home feeling like one whose 'wanderings had lasted many years' (p.477), his intention of returning suggests that his earlier passion for exploring the possibilities of life has been severely compromised. This is apparent in the difference between his obsession with Estella and his pragmatic decision to marry Biddy. The benefits of Pip's youthful success can only really be seen by comparing the young Pip to his middle-aged self. The young Pip's voice is vital, spontaneous and free; the older Pip's voice is usually cautious, sanctimonious and clichéd. By losing the opportunity to become a great man and being forced to settle for a modest career, Pip is cheated of his Expectations.

Interpretation 2

Everything that Pip achieves after inheriting his fortune is debased, false or illusory. Barring small exceptions – his willingness to help out Herbert, for example – the money Pip inherits strips him of all the positive qualities that he had built up in his formative years. Although he recovers these at the end, to an extent, he is changed forever by the bad effects of his good fortune.

A warning sign exists in the parallels between Pip's personality and the personality of those he claims to despise. For example, Pip goes along with Pumblechook's lies even when he knows about his deceit, dining with the impostor when he will not dine with Joe, to whom he owes virtually everything.

But it is the power of money itself that makes Pip into a worse person. Unable or unwilling to interact with other people in a normal manner, Pip instead uses them as tools to achieve his own ends. Money, he discovers, is the best tool of all for turning people into objects. Instead of being sympathetic towards people less fortunate than himself after he becomes wealthy, Pip turns brutal. He is delighted to receive preferential treatment from Trabb the tailor and gloats that his money had 'morally laid upon his back, Trabb's boy' (p.152), an acquaintance from his youth who is now forced to do Pip's bidding.

Pip has a similarly unequal relationship with his servant. This boy, who is named 'Pepper', is rechristened 'the Avenger' by Pip and is the subject of many of Pip's cruel taunts. Pip, it seems, simply enjoys using his money to make the lives of others more difficult. The servant's mocking nickname is given without any good reason on Pip's part, and at no time does his behaviour justify Pip's contempt. Pip, of course, hates his servant because he represents everything that Pip wishes to reject from his old life. From the beginning, this servant is a mere possession to him. Worse, Pip physically abuses the Avenger just as he was abused when he was a boy: 'I went so far as to seize the Avenger by his blue collar and shake him off his feet, – so that he was actually in the air, like a booted Cupid, – for presuming to suppose that we wanted a roll' (p.275).

In Pip's hands, wealth becomes a means of control, turning Pip into a kind of mini-megalomaniac whose only relation to others is through power. This happens in subtle ways as well as obvious ones: guilty at not seeing Joe on his return to his village, Pip sends him 'a barrel of oysters' (p.246), an unconscionably cold act towards someone who raised him as a child. The only thing Pip gains from his wealth is a sense of entitlement. When he loses this, he laments to Herbert that he is 'fit for nothing' (p.342). And it is true. By compelling him to quit his honest trade and become an idle person who lives off the labour of others, Pip's money has turned him into a shell of himself. The final return to the forge, which echoes that of the Prodigal Son, is his only hope of clawing back a decent existence by making amends to the decent people he has wronged.

QUESTIONS & ANSWERS

Essay writing – an overview

An essay is a formal and serious piece of writing that presents your point of view on the text, usually in response to a given essay topic. Your 'point of view' in an essay is your interpretation of the meaning of the text's language, structure, characters, situations and events, supported by detailed analysis of textual evidence.

Analyse – don't summarise

In your essays it is important to avoid simply summarising what happens in a text:

- A summary is a description or paraphrase (retelling in different words) of the characters and events. For example: 'Macbeth has a horrifying vision of a dagger dripping with blood before he goes to murder King Duncan'.
- An analysis is an explanation of the real meaning or significance that lies 'beneath' the text's words (and images, for a film). For example: 'Macbeth's vision of a bloody dagger shows how deeply uneasy he is about the violent act he is contemplating – as well as his sense that supernatural forces are impelling him to act'.

A limited amount of summary is sometimes necessary to let your reader know which part of the text you wish to discuss. However, always keep this to a minimum and follow it immediately with your analysis (explanation) of what this part of the text is really telling us.

Plan your essay

Carefully plan your essay so that you have a clear idea of what you are going to say. The plan ensures that your ideas flow logically, that your argument remains consistent and that you stay on the topic. An essay plan should be a list of **brief dot points** – no more than half a page. It includes:

- your central argument or main contention – a concise statement (usually in a single sentence) of your overall response to the topic. See 'Analysing a sample topic' for guidelines on how to formulate a main contention.
- three or four dot points for each paragraph indicating the main idea and evidence/examples from the text. Note that in your essay you will need to *expand* on these points and *analyse* the evidence.

Structure your essay

An essay is a complete, self-contained piece of writing. It has a clear beginning (the introduction), middle (several body paragraphs) and end (the last paragraph or conclusion). It must also have a central argument that runs throughout, linking each paragraph to form a coherent whole.

See examples of introductions and conclusions in the 'Analysing a sample topic' and 'Sample answer' sections.

The introduction establishes your overall response to the topic. It includes your main contention and outlines the main evidence you will refer to in the course of the essay. Write your introduction *after* you have done a plan and *before* you write the rest of the essay.

The body paragraphs argue your case – they present evidence from the text and explain how this evidence supports your argument. Each body paragraph needs:

- a strong topic sentence (usually the first sentence) that states the main point being made in the paragraph
- evidence from the text, including some brief quotations
- analysis of the textual evidence explaining its significance and explanation of how it supports your argument
- links back to the topic in one or more statements, usually towards the end of the paragraph.

Connect the body paragraphs so that your discussion flows smoothly. Use some linking words and phrases like 'similarly' and 'on the other hand', though don't start every paragraph like this. Another strategy is to use a significant word from the last sentence of one paragraph in the first sentence of the next.

Use key terms from the topic – or synonyms for them – throughout, so the relevance of your discussion to the topic is always clear.

The conclusion ties everything together and finishes the essay. It includes strong statements that emphasise your central argument and provide a clear response to the topic.

Avoid simply restating the points made earlier in the essay – this will end on a very flat note and imply that you have run out of ideas and vocabulary. The conclusion is meant to be a logical extension of what you have written, not just a repetition or summary of it. Writing an effective conclusion can be a challenge. Try using these tips:

- Start by linking back to the final sentence of the second-last paragraph – this helps your writing to 'flow', rather than just leaping back to your main contention straight away.
- Use synonyms and expressions with equivalent meanings to vary your vocabulary. This allows you to reinforce your line of argument without being repetitive.
- When planning your essay, think of one or two broad statements or observations about the text's wider meaning. These should be related to the topic and your overall argument. Keep them for the conclusion, since they will give you something 'new' to say but still follow logically from your discussion. The introduction will be focused on the topic, but the conclusion can present a wider view of the text.

Essay topics

1. How does Pip's life story challenge the connection between material success and personal happiness?
2. 'Pip's story suggests that trying to improve your own situation in life is futile.' Discuss.
3. '*Great Expectations* is a story about a selfish person who learns to love others.' Discuss.
4. '*Great Expectations*' rejection of the romantic idea of true love means that Pip and Estella could never be happy together.' Do you agree?

5 *'Great Expectations* demonstrates that most people will always act according to their own self-interest.' Do you agree?

6 *'Great Expectations* offers an essentially pessimistic view of human nature.' Discuss.

7 How does Pip's personality change during the course of the novel?

8 'In *Great Expectations,* Dickens paints a bleak picture of a society that crushes the weak and rewards the strong.' Discuss.

9 'Pip's futile quest for glory suggests that most people's dreams are unachievable.' Discuss.

10 'Despite its dark themes, *Great Expectations* ultimately offers hope that love will triumph over hatred.' Do you agree?

Vocabulary for writing on *Great Expectations*

Antihero: A protagonist who does not possess many positive values, and whose personality often forms a critique of their society.

Bildungsroman: A novel about the development of a young person into maturity.

Irony: A critical form of humour similar to sarcasm, created when an idea is expressed that is the opposite of what is actually the case.

Repression: A process by which a feeling is blocked out of a person's consciousness, often because that particular feeling is deemed unacceptable by society.

Social advancement: The process of moving from one class to a more wealthy class.

Analysing a sample topic

How does Pip's life story challenge the connection between material success and personal happiness?

This question asks you to explain how the novel challenges a belief – in this case, the idea that material success will bring happiness. You could argue *against* the topic, and claim that that the novel does *not* challenge the money = happiness equation. However, as the question is worded to give support to a particular viewpoint, you should at least consider agreeing with the topic in some respects.

Consider the evidence

By asking how the novel challenges a particular view, the question gives you the chance to offer a nuanced position, agreeing with some aspects of each side of the argument. You could argue, for instance, that the novel challenges the simplistic idea that money will automatically generate happiness, while also arguing that the novel presumes that *some* money is necessary for happiness. You don't *have* to do this, of course – you could come down on one side or the other if you strongly agree or disagree.

You might want to look initially at some examples that support the money = happiness equation. Are there any characters in the novel who *are* made happier by material success, or made happy at certain times of their lives? Consider Pip's excitement when he first leaves for London with the 'world … spread before me' (p.160). It would be a good idea to refer to these moments, even if it is just to add a contrasting point to counterbalance your general agreement with the topic.

Then consider the other side of the argument by looking at whether Pip's unhappiness *increases* in some ways when he becomes rich. This will involve gathering evidence from various elements of Pip's adolescent life: When does he tell us that he is unhappy? What reasons does he give for this?

Sample introduction

> After an initial burst of happiness and excitement when he first learns of his Expectations, Pip's happiness goes into steady and permanent decline. While Pip believes that his good fortune has given him true freedom, he soon realises that his inheritance has come at the expense of his contentment. Rather than liberating him, Pip's suddenly changed financial circumstances thrust him into a life of exile and isolation from

which he struggles to return. His wealth forces him away from the one environment where he was ever remotely happy, and which he is unable to fully rejoin even as an adult.

Body paragraph 1

- Briefly discuss Pip's childhood ambition to become rich, and explain his justification for this wish.
- Look at the stifling limits of his early life and explain how the opportunity of escape from these confines could seem like an attractive proposition.
- Also look at the first time – that is, at Miss Havisham's – that Pip becomes aware of a world outside his own.

Body paragraph 2

- Look at how Pip's habits and concerns begin to change after he enters London as a man of independent means.
- This discussion could deal with evidence of the development of Pip's decadent habits, which could be contrasted with the physical work involved in the first stage of his life.
- It could acknowledge the thrill that Pip gets from being able to spend money, but balance this against his ever-present sense of guilt.

Body paragraph 3

- This could go into slightly darker territory by looking at how Pip's emotional life begins to crumble, which is evident in his cruel treatment of others.
- It could centre on the idea that Pip's desire for wealth is connected to his desire for power, which causes him to dominate others rather than treat them as equals.
- This could in turn be linked to Pip's being unable to form fulfilling relationships with others. Pip now only wants things that he cannot have, meaning that he is unable to find contentment.

Body paragraph 4

- Combine these points in order to draw the conclusion that Pip's wealth, by loosening his bond with reality and making his desires insatiable, actually shifts him further and further away from the possibility of a happy existence.
- Explain how the unwelcome revelation of the source of his wealth forces Pip to readjust his goals so that they are more in accordance with reality.

Sample conclusion

> On balance, Pip's success makes him unhappy. His wealth does not enable him to achieve his main aim in life – winning the hand of Estella – and it also prevents his natural process of growth, which only resumes after he realises that his money is tainted. Much of the misery Pip suffers, especially his conviction that he is worthless if he is not successful, stems from the unhealthy belief that money, rather than love, can buy happiness. When this falsehood is finally revealed, Pip must learn virtually from scratch how to form relationships with others, which is the only true source of happiness in the novel.

SAMPLE ANSWER

'In its emphasis on destructive relationships, *Great Expectations* offers an essentially pessimistic view of human nature.' Discuss.

Although *Great Expectations* depicts numerous failed and dysfunctional relationships, the novel is at heart optimistic about humanity. Although many characters demonstrate their capacity for exploitation and hypocrisy, the common thread of friendship running through the story suggests a far more positive picture. While Pip's idea of achieving a 'perfect' union with Estella is self-destructive and unachievable, this aim is eventually replaced with a more realistic view based on developing lasting bonds with others.

It is true that there are many negative, even dysfunctional, relationships portrayed in the novel. One of the most important of these is Miss Havisham's relationship with Estella. Miss Havisham's idea of how to treat others has been corrupted by a traumatic event in her past, when the trust she placed in another person was utterly betrayed. In an unjust act of retaliation, she attempts to transfer her pain onto Pip and Estella – two innocent people. The fact that Miss Havisham's inexcusable manipulations succeed in distorting Estella's personality and breaking Pip's heart may seem to support the idea that the novel lacks faith in humanity.

However, Dickens' belief in the healing power of redemption demonstrates his bedrock faith in the eventual triumph of love over hatred. While the characters who are incapable of change must suffer retribution, all of the important relationships in the novel that have been broken are eventually repaired. Joe's vivid image of life as 'many partings welded together' can be seen as a powerful metaphor for Dickens' faith in the tendency of the positive aspects of human nature to 'weld together' those who have been temporarily pushed apart by human weakness.

Great Expectations offers several powerful examples of positive human relationships to counterbalance its negative ones. The novel's most enduring friendship – that between Joe and Pip – can be seen as an antidote to the cloyingly false friendship between Pip and Pumblechook. Just as Pumblechook cravenly desires Pip's money, Joe is utterly indifferent to it, modestly telling Pip that he feels 'wrong out of the forge, the kitchen, or off th' meshes'. And while Pip abandons Joe after gaining his fortune, Joe (unlike Pumblechook, who disappears immediately) is there to support Pip long after the fortune has evaporated, offering a model of forbearance from which Pip learns a valuable lesson.

The example of Biddy also provides a vision of a positive love between two people, which balances Pip's destructive and one-sided pursuit of Estella. Although Pip does not marry Biddy in the end, his growing affection for her suggests the possibility of a more constructive relationship than he has been capable of previously. Biddy is 'overjoyed', 'touched' and 'proud' to see Pip return at the end of the story, despite his earlier condescension towards her and Joe. Joe and Biddy's reacceptance of Pip, in a perfect example of unconditional love and forgiveness, overshadows and outlasts the negative human relationships portrayed earlier.

The events of the final part of the book are set in motion by true acts of friendship. Pip's original act of kindness towards Magwitch on the marshes is the clearest example of this: despite his knowledge that he will be condemned for helping an escaped convict, he allows his human compassion to override his natural (and understandable) fear of punishment. Similarly, Pip 'closes the circle' by helping Magwitch a second time. His final good deed towards Magwitch is particularly admirable: although repulsed by the convict, Pip again helps Magwitch according to his moral principles.

Several other instances of selflessness suggest that Pip's act was not unique. Pip and Herbert's protection of Magwitch, even at the risk of their own lives, suggests that they are acting without any thought of the possible costs to themselves. Also, Pip is rescued from Orlick by Trabb's boy, who had been humiliated by Pip in the past. These gestures, which occur despite the fact that the characters do not owe anything to those they rescue, suggest an optimistic view of people's capacity for love and compassion that is not always obvious in the text's bleaker sections.

The final chapters reinstate a fundamentally optimistic view of human relationships. We are presented with Joe and Biddy's marriage as an ideal of human love to be emulated. Their productive union, which results in two children, functions as an example of human possibility. From this ending, we can conclude that although Dickens was realistic about people's capacity for failure, he recognised that decent people are capable of genuine love for others.

REFERENCES & READING

Text

Dickens, Charles 2003 (1860–61), *Great Expectations*, Penguin Classics, London.

References

Brooks, Peter 1999, 'Repetition, Repression, and Return: The Plotting of *Great Expectations*', in Edgar Rosenberg, ed., *Great Expectations: Norton Critical Edition*, WW Norton & Co., New York, pp.679–89.

Forster, EM 1955, *Aspects of the Novel*, Harcourt Brace, New York.

Gilmour, Robin 1999, 'The Pursuit of Gentility', in Edgar Rosenberg, ed., *Great Expectations: Norton Critical Edition*, WW Norton & Co., New York, pp.576–82.

Ginsburg, Michael 1999, 'Dickens and the Uncanny: Repression and Displacement in *Great Expectations*', in Edgar Rosenberg, ed., *Great Expectations: Norton Critical Edition*, WW Norton & Co., New York, pp.698–704.

Gissing, George 1999, 'Dickens' Shrews', in Edgar Rosenberg, ed., *Great Expectations: Norton Critical Edition*, WW Norton & Co., New York, pp.627–9.

Hood, Roger 2002, *The Death Penalty*, Oxford University Press, Oxford.

House, Humphrey 1999, 'Pip's Upward Mobility', in Edgar Rosenberg, ed., *Great Expectations: Norton Critical Edition*, WW Norton & Co., New York, pp.572–6.

Hudson, Pat 1998, *The Industrial Revolution*, Oxford University Press, Oxford.

Keating, PJ 1971, *The Working Classes in Victorian Fiction*, Barnes and Noble, New York.

Moynahan, Julian 1999, 'The Hero's Guilt: the Case of *Great Expectations*', in Edgar Rosenberg, ed., *Great Expectations: Norton Critical Edition*, WW Norton & Co., New York, pp.654–63.

Raphael, Linda 1999, 'A Re-Vision of Miss Havisham: Her Expectations and Our Responses', in Edgar Rosenberg, ed., *Great Expectations: Norton Critical Edition*, WW Norton & Co., New York, pp.705–9.

Ricks, Christopher 1999, '*Great Expectations*', in Edgar Rosenberg, ed., *Great Expectations: Norton Critical Edition*, WW Norton & Co., New York, pp.668–74.

Rosenberg, Edgar 1999, 'Launching *Great Expectations*', in Edgar Rosenberg, ed., *Great Expectations: Norton Critical Edition*, WW Norton & Co., New York, pp.389–423.

Sadrin, Anny 1999, 'A Chronology of *Great Expectations*', in Edgar Rosenberg, ed., *Great Expectations: Norton Critical Edition*, WW Norton & Co., New York, pp.537–43.

Shors, Teri 2004, *Understanding Viruses*, Jones and Bartlett, Sudbury, Massachusetts.

Watt, Ian 2001, *The Rise of the Novel*, The University of California Press, Berkeley.

Websites

Convicts to Australia: A Guide to Researching Your Convict Ancestors, members.iinet.net.au/~perthdps/convicts/res-02.html, accessed 14 July 2009.

Daunton, Martin 2004, 'London's "Great Stink" and Victorian Urban Planning', www.bbc.co.uk/history/trail/victorian_britain/social_conditions/victorian_urban_planning_01.shtml, accessed 14 July 2009.

Historical Overview of London Population, LondonOnline, www.londononline.co.uk/factfile/historical, accessed 14 July 2009.

Swift, Simon 2007, 'What the Dickens?', *Guardian*, 18 April, www.guardian.co.uk/books/2007/apr/18/classics.travelnews, accessed 14 July 2009.

For a detailed printable map of Dickens' London, including most of the locations frequented by Pip, see: charlesdickenspage.com/dickens_london_map.html